Addiction

THE  CommonSense
APPROACH

GW00367736

The CommonSense Approach Series

This series of self-help guides from Newleaf provides practical and sound ways to deal with many of life's common complaints.

Each book in the series is written for the layperson, and adopts a commonsense approach to the many questions surrounding a particular topic. It explains what the complaint is, how and why it occurs, and what can be done about it. It includes advice on helping ourselves, and information on where to go for further help. It encourages us to take responsibility for our own health, to be sensible and not always to rely on medical intervention for every ill.

Addiction

THE Common Sense APPROACH

Michael Hardiman

Newleaf

Newleaf

an imprint of

Gill & Macmillan Ltd

Goldenbridge

Dublin 8

with associated companies throughout the world

© Michael Hardiman 1998

0 7171 2707 9

Index compiled by Helen Litton

Design by Identikit Design Consultants, Dublin

Print origination by Carole Lynch

Printed by The Guernsey Press

This book is typeset in Revivial565 9.5pt on 15pt.

A catalogue record for this book is available from the British Library.

1 3 5 4 2

Contents

Foreword

An innate desire to live life with the least amount of pain, and the greatest amount of pleasure, leaves each person vulnerable to addiction. For many, the reality of their lives is painful. Difficulties in relationships, insecurities, poverty, social isolation, personal unhappiness, and the pressures of modern living — all foster a mental tendency to deny or escape the awareness of pain and discomfort.

In Ireland, it is estimated that there may be as many as 100,000 alcoholics, up to 8,000 drug addicts, and many more addicted to nicotine, gambling and other activities that serve to numb the pain of reality. An escape into total elation through alcohol is seen in its pride of place in celebrating, commemorating and ritualising life's events.

In this regard, Michael Hardiman's *Addiction: The CommonSense Approach* is a very valuable resource for all those ill-informed about the nature of addiction, the extraordinary ease with which individuals become imprisoned by it, and its complex passage of distortion and destruction in the lives of both those who become addicted and of their families.

Its publication is important in making simple and accessible that which is generally considered to be a very complex issue. The author shows a keen determination to, on one hand, address the subject of addiction with great sensitivity, clarity and thoroughness; and on the other, to reach into the heart of the matter to bear witness in simple language to the struggle and suffering of those addicted.

The importance of recognising the unique nature of, and meaning expressed in, each person's addiction, is very well elaborated. So too are the physical and psychological aspects of addiction, as well as the nature of the spiritual quest, and the yearnings and longing for connection and bliss which drive individuals towards the 'rewards' of alcohol and drugs.

A complex problem deserves many and varied responses from a comprehensive range of professional services. In exploring and examining some of the options for recovery, from self-help programmes to the more specialised treatments, this book is a clear statement that the care of those addicted should not be the preserve of a few specialists. It offers information and guidance on a wide range of recovery options.

The significance of the book lies in its capacity to provide a very accessible account of addiction, at a time when more and more young people are turning to alcohol and drugs, and when there appears to be no stemming the tide in the numbers becoming prisoners of their enslavement to addictive substances and activities. Whilst raising important questions and sounding some challenges, it should prove a reliable and readable resource for the layperson as well as professionals.

Maura Russell
Director, The Rutland Centre
Templeogue, Dublin

CHAPTER 1

What is Addiction?

Introduction

'There's no such thing as addiction. So-called addicts are irresponsible, weak-willed no-goods, who can't look after themselves and who want us to feel sorry for them. I know what they need, and I wouldn't be too slow to show them.' The taxi pulls into the car park of the addiction treatment centre and my friend thanks the taxi driver for the insight. The taxi driver cools down a little, takes his fare and says farewell with a somewhat patronising look. He was probably thinking, 'Poor naïve idealist — the world is full of do-gooders, God help them.'

It is understandable that people can have this opinion of addicts and of those who try to help them. Seeing the destruction caused by addiction can make the onlooker angry and vengeful. Newspapers relate stories of drug addicts beating up old ladies for their pensions. Court reports give accounts of addicts robbing houses in order to feed their habit. Some people have relatives who, in active alcoholism, mistreat their spouses and children. These are the images people have when they hear the word addict. It is small wonder, then, that many come to view addiction as simply the addict's failure to be responsible and have self-control.

One incident comes to mind. Some time back, I was asked to testify on behalf of a compulsive gambler who had embezzled large sums of money and faced prison. I was asked to tell the court about the addictive nature of compulsive gambling. After presenting my report, one of the barristers quipped that the judge was of the old school and unlikely to accept the notion that stealing money to bet on horses was a disease! Even the defendant laughed, and we all agreed it was a lot to ask of someone who had no understanding of this kind of addiction.

So, what is addiction? Is this simple view accurate? Is it merely a matter of some people failing to control certain activities, and causing great harm as a result, or is there some more complex process at work?

What is Addiction?

The term addiction comes from the Latin *ad dicere*, which means 'to give oneself up', or 'over'. Addiction occurs when a person surrenders to a substance or activity, which gradually takes control of his life and eventually destroys him if he does not find recovery. The fact that addiction is an enslavement to some substance or activity is generally accepted by those who work in the area. What is still debated is the manner in which a person becomes enslaved. Why do some people become addicts and others do not? Why do some recover, while others eventually die as a direct, or indirect, result of their addiction? Why do some addicts spend their lives struggling between abstaining and relapsing again and again? All these questions go to the core of the issue: what is the true nature of addiction?

Any useful definition of addiction must include the essential attributes and exclude the others. There appear to be four main components to any addiction, namely compulsion, dependence, regularity and destructiveness. Each of these becomes more and more extreme, as addiction expands and develops in the life of the addict.

Compulsion

A compulsion is a very strong, sometimes overwhelming, desire to do something. The back cover of the latest thriller says, 'Compulsive reading, you won't be able to put it down!' In some cases, this turns out to be true. The addicted individual feels intense desire to use a drug, or act out the addictive behaviour.

Dependence

Dependence is the need to do something, as distinct from a desire to do it. Central to the notion is relying on someone or something. The phrase 'I am depending on you, be there,' means we will feel let down, abandoned or unsupported if that person doesn't turn up. So dependence, as it relates to addiction, is the knowledge or belief that some negative or undesirable result will follow if the person does not take drugs, or act out an addictive behaviour.

Regularity

Regularity means that the addictive behaviour is a consistent feature of the person's life. There can be a great deal of variability among people in terms of the amount of addictive events. The binge drinker may break out only every six months, whereas the alcohol addict who tops up the alcohol level may drink every day. Additionally, the number of addictive events may change as the addiction grows in strength, so what may have begun as a weekly, or fortnightly, event becomes a daily occurrence.

Destructiveness

A fourth essential element in addiction is that of its destructive nature. Destructiveness means causing harm or injury to someone or something. There are varied degrees of destruction. There can be on-going gradual deterioration, or immediate catastrophic injury, and a wide range of possibilities in between.

Defining Addiction

Combining these elements, we can reach a definition of addiction as a condition whereby an individual regularly takes a substance, or acts in a particular way, in response to a strong and sometimes overwhelming desire to do so; and that in the absence of so doing, he will experience negative feelings or actual illness. By taking the substance or carrying out the behaviour, the addict causes harm to himself or others.

Using this definition, addicts are involved in doing something that is harmful to themselves or others in response to a strong desire to do so, and a fear of what will happen if they don't. This approach implies that addicts are not simply irresponsible people, but that they are responding to very strong driving forces behind their addictive behaviours.

Furthermore, it implies that addiction is not an all-or-nothing phenomenon. It is impossible to draw a line between addiction and non-addiction. In general, becoming addicted is a gradual process, measured by the intensity of the compulsions, the depth of dependence and the degree of destructiveness. Thus, one person can be mildly addicted to something, and another can be very strongly addicted to the same thing. The intensity of addiction is often related to the nature of the substance or activity, and the length of time the individual has been involved with it.

Summary

Thus far, we are being purely descriptive of the nature of addiction. Looked at in this manner, it is clear that everybody is a potential addict, and maybe most of us are in some way involved in addictive behaviour. So, the reader may ask, what is my addiction? Some addictions are much more destructive than others, and some people progress far down the road of the more dangerous addictions. It is these people, who destroy their own lives and damage others, whom we tend to identify as true addicts.

To help treat and heal these lives, and minimise the damage, it is important to understand the nature of the problem. Addiction has four main parts: 1. the nature of the driving forces that produce addiction; 2. the psychological states of the addicted person; 3. the variety of addictive substances or behaviours; and 4. the process by which recovery occurs. The remainder of this book addresses these issues.

CHAPTER 2

The Causes of Addiction

Introduction

Much controversy has surrounded this topic over the past few decades. Some view addiction as a disease that overtakes some people, but not others — a kind of genetic time bomb, that lies dormant within the biological make-up of the addict until it is triggered off by ingesting a chemical. Psychologists and social workers tend to emphasise the social and psychological aspects of addiction, seeing it as a response to emotional dysfunction or social impoverishment. Those with a religious focus may see it as moral failure and the basic sinfulness of humankind.

This chapter examines the constellation of causes involved in why certain people become addicted and others do not. The key point here is that there is no one cause for addiction — looking for a single cause to such a complex and widespread human phenomenon is pointless.

Addiction is fast becoming the main social health care issue of modern society. Every generation has had a key social health problem. At the turn of the century, there was destitution wrought by urbanisation and the industrial revolution. Disease was rampant in densely populated slums, where bad hygiene, little medicine and an uncaring elite left thousands to their fate.

Two world wars in a forty-year period cost millions of lives and destroyed many European countries, making it difficult to see any social health trend developing until the peaceful era of the 1950s. Since then, with economic expansion, the problem of addiction has grown and spread throughout most Western societies. Addiction is like a cancer that spreads throughout the human family. And like cancer it will take a lot of research to prevent its spread and to treat those afflicted. A crucial step in this process is the question: what causes addiction? If we know the causes, then we can begin to look for solutions.

The Causes of Addiction

Gordon Allport, one of the founding fathers of psychology, offered a brilliant insight into human behaviour with the term 'functional autonomy'. By this, he means that some human behaviour can be caused by a set of forces or events, but the behaviour can continue for reasons other than those that gave rise to it in the first place. I think this notion is vital to understanding the link between the causes of addiction and the forces that keep addiction going. The original causes may not be the forces that sustain addiction. Thus, there are two distinct dimensions, the original causes and the sustaining forces. This chapter examines the first aspect.

There are at least three key elements involved in why people become addicted: 1. the nature of the addicting substance; 2. the powerful motive forces behind some people's need to alter their internal emotional experience, or to put it more simply, to change their mood artificially; 3. the individual's physical vulnerability to addictive substances.

The beginning of all addiction is a combination of these three elements. Let's look at each of them more closely.

The Nature of the Substance

Certain substances are powerfully addictive in themselves, and we need look no further than the exposure to the substance itself to explain why a person becomes addicted. These substances affect the body chemistry, usually the central nervous system, leading to a mood change. How addictive they are depends on several things — the speed at which they affect the body chemistry, the way the body adapts to their presence, the experience they produce, and the speed at which they leave the body. Substances that act quickly and are quick to leave the body are the most addictive. Nicotine, for example, is so highly addictive a substance that we need not look elsewhere for the cause of cigarette smoking other than exposure to the drug itself.

Most people try cigarette smoking as teenagers. After a few initial upsets — coughing, dizziness, nausea — the body adapts and the individual becomes quickly hooked to the stimulant drug, nicotine. The drug enters the bloodstream via the lungs, and goes quickly to the brain. It takes about thirty minutes to start clearing from the system, which leads to withdrawal pangs and a desire to smoke again. This is why many people smoke an average of twenty cigarettes a day. While this is a good example of chemical addiction, other addictions are not so easily understood.

Altering Mood

Human beings desire pleasure and avoid pain. Most healthy activities also make us feel good. Eating, sex, rest and exercise are all basic physical activities that provide pleasurable sensations. Achievement, praise and affection are psychological equivalents that are also pleasurable. Conversely, painful experiences often accompany dangerous events or behaviours. Getting too close to an open fire causes a mild burning sensation, which helps us to avoid a serious burn. Going too long without food causes hunger pangs. Not enough love leaves a feeling of loneliness. These painful experiences help us to avoid danger and to seek what we need to be healthy. Every human being is, therefore, to some extent, pursuing pleasure and avoiding pain. Addiction is a good example of what happens when this process becomes distorted or unbalanced.

Addicts, in general, begin by using some substance or behaviour in an inappropriate way to produce pleasure or avoid pain, thus affecting their emotional state. The kinds of experience sought after are many and varied but they have one thing in common: a desire to repeat the experience. There are four general kinds of such experience: (i) creating a feeling of elation or excitement; (ii) relieving anxiety or some other emotional pain; (iii) creating a feeling of power or confidence; (iv) and creating a feeling of connection or unity. Let us examine each in turn.

Elation and Excitement

I remember the day that the Republic of Ireland soccer team got through to the quarter-finals of the world cup. The team drew nil-all with Romania, and the game went to a penalty shoot-out. I sat with friends in a pub in Cork and the atmosphere was electric. With the last of the five penalties, the Irish goalkeeper dived right and palmed the ball away. The pub exploded — people were singing, dancing, hugging each other in a pure and unrestrained exhilarated expression of joy. We were high. It was a very exciting experience, and one that gave some idea of the seductive attraction of any event, or substance, that can make someone feel so good.

Certain chemicals (mainly stimulants), and certain activities (e.g. compulsive gambling), can produce feelings of great elation and pleasure. It is easy to understand the temptation to repeat them. People enslaved to the need for elation and excitement are one particular set of addicts. They often have difficulties with responsibility, a low tolerance for endurance and are somewhat immature in their development. They differ from those who use drugs or addictive behaviour to ease and repress painful feelings. This leads to a very important observation about addiction. Every addict has a particular preference for certain substances or behaviours. The 'drug of choice' is determined by the kind of experience sought. Thus, there are many reasons why certain addicts are attracted to particular kinds of experiences. Taking account of these reasons is an essential element in assisting long-term recovery for addicts. The second type of mood alteration is that of relieving painful feelings.

Relieving Emotional Pain

A very common cause of addiction is the use of chemicals, or addictive behaviour, to relieve emotional pain. Prescription drugs such as Valium and other sedative chemicals, including alcohol, are more often the choice when this is the underlying purpose. Addictive activities such as self-mutilation and eating disorders are also related to a need to relieve internal emotional pain.

A colleague and I were talking recently about judgmental attitudes to some poorer people who spend their welfare payments on drink, instead of feeding their families. In general, these people are judged harshly and criticised for their failure. On reflection, however, let us imagine their situation. The world for many of these people is one without opportunity, where long-term unemployment leaves a sense of betrayal and boredom, where many do not have the skills to change their lives, and where love, hope and intimacy are seen mostly on television, having died long ago under the weight of poverty and lack of relationship skills.

Along comes a drug that can be bought legally and a place where it can be taken; where the dartboard, the pool table and the camaraderie all combine to relieve boredom, to enhance warm feelings of connection to others, to relieve feelings of helplessness and desperation. It is easy to understand the seductive power of this drug, and why so many fall foul to its ministrations and become addicts.

This is only one of many possible images that illustrate the point that many addicts are trying to relieve some kind of pain. They unfortunately end up dependent on a substance that only makes things worse, and which in turn increases the need for the drug. Thus, the crippling cycle — pain, relief or escape, more pain, more relief — continues until finally destruction follows. This is common in many forms of addiction.

Creating a Feeling of Power and Confidence

Eminent psychologist, Alfred Adler, considered that the need for power is a fundamental driving force in people. Much of my experience suggests that he is correct. There are many meanings of the word power. Here, it refers to the ability to exert influence on the course of one's life. Without some sense of power, we become helpless pawns, pushed hither and thither, dominated and used for other people's ends.

I have been fascinated at the way the many powerless people become fodder for those who exert power. Childhood experiences are a major influence in why a person becomes powerless. This sense of powerlessness is revealed in adult life in the following ways: being unable to solve problems and to create an individual life; an attraction to people you can depend on for direction; being unable to make decisions for oneself; and an inability to leave situations that are hurtful or damaging.

Lack of initiative is rooted in the belief that nothing you do makes any difference. People like this feel that life happens to them. They take little responsibility, and are often directionless. Instead of developing into adults with a sense of what they wish to do with their lives, they sit back and let somebody else make decisions for them. They are drawn to people who like to take control. Early on, there is comfort in having someone, or some system of belief, to give direction on how to live. Eventually, this leads to a growing sense of helplessness. To live healthy and fulfilling lives, we must be able to exert some degree of power over our environment. Those who become powerless are almost always damaged by the experience.

Into this context let us introduce a drug, such as cocaine, or some of the hallucinogens that give a feeling of superiority, omnipotence and/or a deep experience of being in control. When such drugs wear off, the feelings of powerlessness are greater, and may even become more extreme by feelings of fear and anxiety. This complicating of the emotional needs often leads to cross addiction (i.e. addiction to different types of substances). An individual might use, for example, an opiate such as heroin, to help cope with the emotional crash from drugs that are used to produce feelings of power, and then gradually become addicted to heroin.

Creating a Feeling of Connection or Unity

Thus far, we have discussed drugs in relation to emotional needs; these needs can be considered to belong to the worlds of self and others, and include excitement, pain relief and power. Another set of needs that often underlies the use of certain drugs or activities can be thought to belong to the spiritual realm, namely the relation to the cosmos. The needs that lie behind the use of these drugs are spiritual.

People have always experienced altered states of consciousness. These occur when their awareness of the here and now becomes obsolete, and is overtaken by a set of internal experiences usually of a dramatic nature. This can be described as unity consciousness. At such times, many individuals claim to have met God, or to have had an experience of becoming one with the universe. Central to this is losing the sense of one's own individual identity, an overriding sense of peace, and a feeling that all is well and that you are part of a great purpose.

Historically, one group of people were marked out as being particularly blessed with these experiences and were considered mystics. Techniques such as meditation, breathing, drumming and so on were used, sometimes with drugs, to enhance these experiences. In general, the individuals who embarked on these mystical journeys to the interior realms of the soul were held in respect and awe by others in the community.

The altered states of consciousness had an important role in the overall spiritual welfare of the community at large.

Today, altered states of consciousness have lost their cultural and religious mooring. Additionally, more and more chemicals are available that can create this state quickly for people who take them. Alongside these changes, we have seen massive growth in a materialistic and consumer driven ethos, which denies the importance of the sacred and elevates the secular. Orthodox religions have lost much of their credibility, and are less able to direct the spiritual growth of those in their care. These changes have left an enormous spiritual vacuum.

Some people do not understand the nature of this spiritual crisis. Perhaps all they experience is a deep sense of ennui, or alienation. Into this widespread spiritual hunger they bring hallucinogenic substances, or the opiates, or some well packaged meditative technique. The scene is then set for many people to be seduced into a counterfeit spirituality that leaves them ultimately spiritually bankrupt, physically injured, and in many cases emotionally destroyed.

Physical Make-Up

One area of controversy in the study of addiction is the role a person's physical make-up plays in whether or not they become addicted. Some people seem to be more prone to chemical addiction than others. This vulnerability to addiction is related to the way their brain chemistry interacts with addictive substances, and may be genetically inherited. There is a continuing search for medication to treat the chemistry of the brain, so as to reduce, or get rid of, its need for addictive substances. Presently, there are drugs on the market — or being developed — that treat the craving for alcohol, nicotine, heroin and cocaine.

There is a physical component in addiction, and chemical addiction is profoundly physical in nature. The question is whether or not the addiction is physically dormant within the person, awaiting the ingesting of a substance that sets off its progress. Can a person be an addict before they take a drug? Is a person an alcoholic before taking a drink? In relation to any particular individual, there is, in my opinion, no definitive answer to this question. Certain people, who inherit a vulnerability to addiction, never become addicts; others, with no family or genetic tendency, can and do become addicted. And, as we saw earlier, taking certain drugs will lead to addiction no matter what physical, or psychological, forces are at work. The best we can do is accept that statistically, more people with a physical vulnerability to addiction will become addicted than will those who do not have such a vulnerability.

Summary

This chapter has briefly examined the causes of addiction, and has shown that all addiction involves using some substance or activity to alter a person's experience, and, in the case of chemical addiction, the drug interacts with body chemistry. Furthermore, different kinds of experience determine the drug or behaviour that is used. The person's need to create certain experiences, and relying on addictive substances to do so, can not be separated from their social/spiritual condition, or psychological and physical make-up. Social conditions, spiritual needs, psychological and physical make-up are vital to understanding the causes of any person's addiction. Understanding the range of causes in the addiction of any individual is crucial for their long-term recovery.

CHAPTER 3

What Sustains Addiction?

Introduction

T his chapter examines some key issues that help us understand why addiction can become so destructive, and also why it is so difficult a problem to solve. Addiction brings about many personality changes; it is not a condition that stabilises, but instead gets progressively worse. It changes the person, gets worse and resists change. We will examine each of these issues in turn.

Early attempts to understand addiction led to a conclusion that there was a certain personality type that could be called an addictive personality. Such people were considered to be emotionally immature, easily frustrated, low in will-power and irresponsible escapists. This view certainly fitted the picture of many who were in treatment for addiction (remember our taxi driver from Chapter 1). There was a serious flaw in this approach, however. Much of what was seen as part of the personality of addicts was a symptom of the addiction, rather than its cause. This realisation led to a closer study of the personality changes that seem to occur as a result of addiction. Several key themes have emerged in this regard; I have categorised these as: falling in love, building defences, chasing the dragon and moral deterioration.

Falling in Love

Perhaps no experience is as dramatic in its effect on people as that wonderfully strange, and often anguished, experience of falling in love. I saw this recently in my work. A young woman, who was quite troubled with her family, came to see me for a number of sessions to help with some of her problems. Her face was mask-like, and she spoke of the most difficult things with the same flat tone of voice as the most ordinary events. She never smiled. I got used to the struggle of trying to help her express herself and let some of her feelings come to the surface. Then one day, she arrived and I could see that despite her usual timidity and quietness, something had changed. She gradually revealed the cause of the change. She had met a young man and was falling for him. Each time she mentioned his name, a smile lit up her features — she became animated and expressive. It reminded me strongly of seeing this effect in a completely different context, that of addiction.

John came to see me soon after discharge from a psychiatric hospital, where he had been treated for severe alcoholism, which, over fifteen years, had almost completely destroyed him. During one session, I asked him to describe the first time he drank. His voice changed, and a softness crept into his features. He held up an imaginary glass and I believe that he could see, in his mind's eye, the light reflecting off the bronze liquid. After a brief moment of quiet reflection, he described that delicious feeling, first encountered through alcohol, which he depicted as having 'tasted the elixir of life'.

Falling in love is like an incredibly intense feeling of coming home to some place that is truly warm, safe, delightful, and which has the illusion of meeting all your needs and healing all your hurts. John's experience of alcohol was, in all its elements, comparable to that experience. This nostalgia and sentiment, common among addicts, is called 'euphoric recall'. Addicts fall in love with their substance, and build an incredibly strong emotional attachment to it.

When we fall in love, certain changes occur (including changes to the chemistry of the brain!). We go slightly insane.

Our thoughts become obsessive and we think of the loved one constantly; we miss them when they are away, and we look forward to the wonderful times ahead, of sharing and loving and holding and healing. Work and friendships can suffer neglect. We idealise the loved one, unable to see any faults, intrigued and charmed by their little idiosyncrasies (which with the passage of time we will grow to dislike, or even resent). And we are so loyal to them, no one is allowed to question the new-found love. The fact that he is broke, seems angry with the world, is irresponsible, or workaholic, or ruthless, or changeable, has no bearing on our love and on the belief that this is it: we have found the one. And so the addict, in falling in love with his substance, has found something to rely on that will make his world better and release him from his struggle. He protects this experience from the cold criticism of others by building a psychological defence structure.

Building Defences

The next personality change occurs when the addict's life begins to come apart, as a direct result of his addiction. These negative consequences cause some readjustments to occur in the psyche of the addict. Eliot Aronson, a social psychologist, comes to our aid in understanding these changes. He discovered — what most of know intuitively — that human beings cannot live comfortably whilst holding two incompatible beliefs. This is called 'cognitive dissonance', and refers to the anxiety that occurs when we are faced with having two beliefs that contradict each other.

Let us look at a few examples. One very obvious one, which will become particularly topical at the turn of the century, is found when certain religious expectations, or prophecies, of the end of the world fail to come true. Many have travelled out to remote places to watch the apocalypse, only to have to drive home disappointed. Their sacred scriptures and leaders, inspired by God, told them it would happen — but it didn't. Now they are left in a dilemma: how can someone inspired by God be wrong? This kind of inner conflict is called cognitive dissonance. One belief — inspired by God — is dissonant with the other — 'getting it wrong'.

Addiction creates one of the most intense forms of cognitive dissonance, namely: how can a substance or activity that I love so much, need so badly, and depend on so heavily, be so bad for me? In coping with this conflict, many addicts go through major changes in personality. To understand addiction and recovery, we need to examine these changes.

Aronson's work can be used to explain why addicts go to such lengths to defend themselves. Freudian psychology, on the other hand, tells how the addict raises this defence. Combining these two, we can see that addicts develop an elaborate, distorted way of seeing things that allows them to withstand the anxiety and pain of facing up to the effects of their addiction. This distorted system is constructed by using several psychological strategies, which are called defence mechanisms.

Freud recognised defence mechanisms as part of normal personality functioning. They are not in themselves dangerous, and are often important tools in coping with difficult and traumatic situations. They become problematic, however, when consistently relied upon as a means of blocking out reality, rather than as their normal function, which is to give the individual enough time to come to terms with a problem and become psychologically prepared for change.

In addiction, defence mechanisms become an intrinsic part of the addictive process. The defence mechanisms used by addicts are no different from those used by most people, but they are used in a dysfunctional manner. Several key defence mechanisms that occur in most addiction are: denial, rationalisation, minimisation, projection and displacement.

Denial

Denial is the 'belle of the ball' of defence mechanisms, and it can be defined as the inability to see a problem as real. It is not simply a matter of lying to oneself, or to others (although lying can be part of denial). Rather, it is psychological blindness. A very common example is the initial reaction that many people have to bereavement. The telephone rings, a person answers and is told by a relative that their mother has died. After hanging up the telephone, the person walks around in a daze, and begins to find a set of possibilities that might explain the information, other than the reality of the death. The person may live in this denial state for a short time, or may remain in it for years. In relation to bereavement, the initial purpose of denial is to help the individual prepare for the sometimes overwhelming feelings of grief that follow the loss of a loved one.

Addiction usually brings an increase in the use of denial by the addict, in order to protect himself from the negative consequences of addiction. He does not believe that there is a problem, and will explain it in a whole variety of ways. Additionally, his drug use may interfere with his perception of reality, so he may not even have evidence for the problem.

Everyone else may see the obvious problems — ill health, missed work, wild mood changes, inappropriate and/or dangerous behaviour. Whilst the addict may deny all this, he may not even have the same information as others, due to the effect of chemicals. A classic example is that of the alcoholic black-out. Black-outs occur when a person drinks to the point where experiences are not recorded by the brain in the normal way. Often the events that happen during the black-out period can only be recalled when the person gets intoxicated again.

'The morning after the night before' may dawn on the partner of an alcoholic as a bleak experience, as she remembers her partner ogling the hostess and making blatant sexual innuendoes whilst inebriated. Her partner denies it, saying it wasn't so bad and was all in good fun. The reality is that he can't remember the event, and doesn't want to admit this, because it only further fuels her conviction that he has a drink problem.

Rationalisation

Rationalisation is a common defence mechanism which has, as its central element, the giving of logical reasons for inappropriate behaviour (a more sophisticated version of making excuses). Nobody wants to feel foolish or out of control. And most of us use rationalisation as a means of protecting ourselves when we make mistakes.

Let's take a very simple, everyday example. You are walking along absent-mindedly and suddenly trip over yourself. For a brief moment, you are out of control, lose your balance and look somewhat foolish. Your immediate reaction is to look at the ground with puzzled intensity, to discover what has tripped you. A large part of this is to provide yourself and onlookers with a rational explanation for your clumsy behaviour. In most instances, it is not a matter of the ground being at fault, but there is comfort in believing it to be so. Rationalisation is quite a common, and often useful, method of defending one's ego. In addiction, however, its use becomes extreme and very destructive, as it allows addicts to explain away many of the destructive elements of their behaviour.

In the early stages of addiction, the reasons given for addictive behaviour can have a ring of truth. The person in early-stage anorexia, for example, can give compelling reasons for losing weight. Dress size and the economics of her wardrobe, as well as the need to be healthy, can all be a reasonable facade to cover a growing obsession with food and losing weight. It can be difficult to argue with these seemingly plausible reasons for the dieting and exercising in early-stage anorexia. It becomes more difficult to hear these same explanations used by an emaciated figure, whose body is deteriorating from the effects of starvation.

Similarly, early-stage alcohol addiction comes with a fairly common set of plausible reasons. A person who drinks on the way home every night may say it helps him to relax and be in better shape to tend to his family when he gets home. Another can say that drink helps him to gain confidence. A woman who works in the home may believe that her mid-morning gin and tonic gives her the energy she needs to keep house. Rationalisation is primarily used, not to convince others of the reasonableness of addictive pursuits (although that is one feature), but rather to allow the addict to convince himself.

Minimisation

Minimisation is a near relative to denial. Whilst denial works by failure to see or acknowledge a problem, minimisation works by stripping away some of the more difficult and destructive aspects of addictive behaviour, leaving a smaller and not so serious problem. A simple example is found in the ordinary experience of using credit facilities. Many people buy things on credit, because they are able to minimise the difficulties involved in repayment (e.g. it works out at only £5 a week). It could be said that without the use of defence mechanisms on the part of borrowers, many banks would make far less profit!

In addiction, minimisation is developed to a keen level. A recent discussion with a young man heavily psychologically dependent on cannabis, and whose functioning has seriously deteriorated from his drug taking, clarifies this issue. Within moments of asking whether his drug habit is related to his other difficulties, including low tolerance for frustration and almost zero motivation and energy, he minimises the problem. He says he only smokes in the evening (neglecting to say that he doesn't go to bed until 5 a.m.). He is also quick to explain that most of his friends smoke the odd joint (neglecting to discuss one or two who are heavy users), and that furthermore, cannabis is less toxic than nicotine. It is clear that he believes that what he is doing is much less serious than it is. By minimising his use of cannabis, he avoids making the connection between its place in his life and his other problems.

Projection and Displacement

These two defence mechanisms are quite similar. Projection occurs when we see in other people attributes and feelings which we refuse to recognise in ourselves. At the cinema, we are viewing an image projected on to a blank screen. If the film is any good, we forget that we are looking at an image and engage in the story. All of us, to a greater or lesser extent, project things on to other people. An angry person can easily project his anger on to others. His life is continually intruded upon by all the angry people who are out to get him. A frightened person sees danger around every corner. A confident person looks at the same corners and sees interesting opportunities. Most of us, therefore, are consistently engaged in projecting our internal emotional states on to the screen of reality.

Displacement involves taking something that is inside us and putting it where it doesn't belong. A good example of displacement is captured in the following cameo. A man gets into trouble at work and his boss tells him off. As a result, he is very angry with his boss and with himself, but is afraid to express his anger in case he gets into more trouble. On his arrival home, he gets angry with his wife because she hasn't prepared a meal for him. She gets upset at his unfair criticism — after all, she's out working too. She recognises that he is very touchy, so rather than escalate the conflict she says nothing and represses her angry feelings.

Some time later, their son arrives in from play with mud on his jacket (a normal occurrence) and she yells at him. He gets upset, says nothing, goes outside and kicks the cat. This scenario shows the defence mechanism of displacement. In each situation, the individual takes out his or her frustrations on someone who is not at fault.

Projection is almost always a matter of the addicted person blaming others for the problems that are occurring in his life (many of these problems may be the direct result of addictive behaviour). Most addicts are notoriously resentful, and believe that the world is responsible for their unhappiness. Phrases such as, 'if only she would be nicer to me', 'give me more sex', 'nag less', 'talk with me more', then I wouldn't drink, take Valium, overeat, etc., are all classic examples of projection. In each, the individual fails to take responsibility for his own behaviour, and refuses to accept that addictive behaviour is not someone else's fault. The target of projection — be it spouse, friend or relative — can end up in a living hell trying to improve so that the addict will stop.

In addiction, displacement can result in violence and brutality, as the addict takes out his growing frustration on other people. Projection is targeting others as responsible; displacement is the next step, that of punishing them. In some situations, displaced anger is expressed indirectly; the addict who refuses to support his family, for example, may be punishing them. The suicidal teenager may use his death threats as a powerful lever to hurt his parents for imagined wrongs that have led him to fail at school, or at work — when in fact it is his drinking, or drugging, that is at fault. These defence mechanisms can be quite subtle, but each aims to distract from the addictive behaviour. A person in a relationship with an addict can be side-tracked easily if the focus is put on to their deficiencies, rather than on the addict's behaviour.

The above is a rather simplified and brief description of the more common defence mechanisms. Using some combination of these, the addict avoids reality and continues to seek the experiences that the drug, or addictive behaviour, originally gave him, even as his life becomes more and more unmanageable. This illusive search for the high, or fix, is such a feature of addiction that it has its own name in drug folklore — chasing the dragon.

Chasing the Dragon

It is unhelpful to speak of drugs, including illegal substances, as if they have no benefits. We know that certain drugs can make a person feel absolutely wonderful, perhaps more wonderful than any experience they might have in a drug-free state. Sitting around being po-faced when drugs are mentioned is of no help in understanding the lengths to which some people will go to access these experiences. The controversial film, *Trainspotting*, suggested, for example, that the rush from a heroin fix was akin to the best orgasm a person can have, multiplied by a thousand.

For the addict, however, there is a gradual change from the original wonderment of the experience to the desperate struggle to recreate these experiences, even as the person's life becomes more and more painful. Relief from pain can be experienced as pleasurable, and herein lies the seduction of some forms of addiction. The original pleasure is lost forever, but the addict doesn't realise this. In general, the addict fails to recognise that to a large extent his drug use becomes a desperate struggle to avoid the pain of withdrawal. And the relief from withdrawal feels pleasurable. But it is not the pleasure of the original state, and the addict begins a futile search for an illusory naïve experience, one that will forever elude him.

The addicted individual becomes enslaved to a drug-created experience that he protects from the cold and painful focus of reality, whilst he pirouettes between the search for an illusion and the relief from pain. The dance gradually becomes a downward spiral, and the addict can become unrecognisable as the reasonable, accommodating person he once was. This leads on to another feature of the progression of addiction — moral deterioration.

Moral Deterioration

It has become somewhat old-fashioned to speak of morality when discussing addiction. There is a broad consensus amongst the informed that addiction is not a moral problem. This consensus emerged as a direct result of the failure of moral approaches — embodied, for example, in the temperance movement — to substance abuse. Addiction came to be seen as a disorder, or disease, that was unresponsive to moral exhortation, and so it is. Morality is, however, an important element in the story of addiction, not as a punitive, guilt-inducing lever to force the addict into submission, but rather as one of the casualties of addiction itself.

Those who observe people in addiction realise that the moral constraints that hold most of us away from very destructive behaviour are gradually eroded in the personality of the addict. They seem to lose normal moral reasoning, and often behave in ways that are clearly morally wrong. It is difficult for some people to understand this progression. This difficulty arises because we tend to see morality as being a God-given function, residing in the soul, that is somewhat mysterious and less prone to corruption than other elements of personality, such as personal hygiene and good manners. There may be simpler explanations.

Psychologists now recognise that moral development and reasoning is not very different from other aspects of development. It involves a value system that emerges through the emotional bonds between a growing child and the people around him. It has two aspects — intellectual beliefs and emotional connections. Thinking and feeling are central elements of morality. These require the healthy functioning of the central nervous system. Most addictive drugs damage this system, to a greater or lesser extent, and thus affect the person's capacity to function in a morally healthy manner. This is the first part of why addiction damages morality. The second reason lies in the human reaction to pain.

It is common for people to react destructively when they are frightened, or in great trauma. We see evidence for this in reports of people trampled to death by a crowd of decent citizens in a state of panic trying to avoid a fire. Other situations occur where people are killed or beaten for a slice of bread, when people are starving. These and other stories tell us that the need for survival can cause ordinary people to become destructive and aggressive. When we judge those who act aggressively as a result of addiction, we tend not to believe that in similar circumstances we may fare no better.

One recovering heroin addict recounted to me that his experience of withdrawal was like having the worst toothache you could imagine. I thought this a vivid illustration, particularly having recently read an account of a man who shot off half his jaw because of a toothache for which he was unable to receive treatment. Those who do not understand the nature of withdrawal can often underestimate the degree to which most human beings would react to this kind of pain, and the desperate acts that it often produces. I believe that most people would compromise some of their deeply held moral values and rob their nearest friend to avoid such pain. This explanation of the moral deterioration in addiction is unacceptable and distasteful to those who would prefer to believe that addicts are somehow weaker, or less moral, than themselves.

Summary

This chapter examined some of the key changes that occur when people become addicted. These changes allow the disorder to progress by changing the person's view of reality. These changes are extremely difficult to confront, because the insight needed to see them is itself undermined. All addicted individuals use some combination of the defence mechanisms discussed above, and all reflect some combination of the personality changes. These could be called the internal signs of addiction, and are signposts that help is needed. Other signs and symptoms of a more external nature are discussed in the next chapter.

CHAPTER 4

Signs and Symptoms

Introduction

T he changes that occur to an addict's personality are often
matched by certain common behaviour patterns. These
can alert those around the person to the growing destructive
elements of the addiction. Some classic signs are mood swings,
lying, stealing, unexplained absences, physical symptoms and
recurrent illness. If a number of these become a consistent
feature and seem to be out of character, then they can be taken
as evidence for growing addiction. It is important to say at this
point that any one of these situations can occur without a
connection to addiction or substance abuse, so we have to be
careful not to jump to conclusions. This is particularly relevant
in the case of adolescence.

Mood Swings

Everybody experiences changes in mood, and some people who
are lively in temperament may experience a lot of variation
in mood without there being anything wrong. In addiction,
mood changes are generally more extreme, seem to be out of
character and come out of the blue. The highs are higher and
the lows lower. There may be physical aspects to mood changes
— the eyes in particular are tell-tale signs; dilation of the pupils,
and a slightly dazed look, can give a clue to the presence of a
mood altering drug.

Mood swings involving anger are particularly telling. The
individual may show less control, and fly off the handle at the

smallest thing. Violent behaviour and abusive language are a consistent feature of certain addictions, such as alcohol and amphetamines. Paranoia is also indicative of certain drug addictions — heavy marijuana usage, for example. The individual may seem very self-conscious and vigilant.

Loss of control over one's emotions is a general feature of all addictions, and underlies the mood swings. This is often due to the effect of drugs on the central nervous system, as well as resulting from a general increase in frustration and unhappiness.

Lying

Lying is very common, because an addict has to hide the truth from himself and others. Telling lies becomes a part of the addict's lifestyle — he does things that he doesn't want others to know of. The need for money, for example, is often vital, and involves making up stories that allow him to convince others to give him money. Psychological addictions are particularly prone to this behaviour. Compulsive gamblers are always in debt, and borrow from Peter to pay Paul. They tell lies to the bank manager to get loans for spurious projects, and lie to friends to help pay the bank, and so on.

Anorexic sufferers use all kinds of manipulative tricks to convince people that they are not starving themselves. Drinking lots of water before weighing themselves, hiding food, exercising and laxative use in secret all go to make up a life that is full of dishonesty. Eventually, lying becomes so ingrained that the person may find it easier to lie than tell the truth, and starts to lie for no identifiable reason. For those who care for these people, there is often great upset and confusion that such lies are told. For peace of mind, it is important to realise that the lies are not a personal betrayal, but rather a symptom of the addictive disorder, which will come right if the individual gets help.

Stealing

Some people will steal whether they are addicted or not. They do so as a way of life, and are recognised as thieves and criminals. Those who steal in order to feed an addiction are in a different category. Most of us would rob our mother's pension if deeply addicted and in need of a fix. Addictions require financial resources, and drug addiction especially so. Very simple sums help us with this. If there are 1,000 heroin addicts in one city, who on average need £100 per day to feed their habit, this means that £700,000 is required for heroin per week, which totals to £36.4 million per year. This money has to be gained from some source or other, and most heroin addicts have very little money, so they resort to dealing in drugs, or stealing. This aspect of addiction leads to enormous levels of crime.

Other addictions also lead to financial problems. Every small town has its examples of people who drank away large inheritances and ended up destitute. Others drank or gambled away successful businesses. Gamblers sometimes end up in jail for embezzlement. The relatively new addiction to telephone sex-lines has led some unfortunates to run up bills so large that they end up re-mortgaging their house to pay them. People who cannot afford to finance their addiction will find some way, legal or not, to get money. Small wonder, then, that stealing is a feature of many addictions. In this sense, the adolescent who steals money for cigarettes is no different from the person who shoplifts to pay for heroin. The stealing is all part of addiction.

Unexplained Absences

When someone is gradually being overtaken by addiction, his life goes out of control. The regular predictability of life is lost. Late hours are kept, and he arrives home later and later in the small hours of the morning. Perhaps he doesn't come home at all. Days are missed from work, and spurious excuses become less and less believable. Teenagers can miss school, play truant or be unable to get up in the morning as a direct result of toxic sedation of the body. The inability to function to a normal timetable is sometimes a telling sign of advanced addiction. This is so because work is often the last thing to go. It pays for the supply of alcohol or other substance, and will be held on to for dear life. Most working addicts cannot afford to lose their jobs.

Physical Symptoms

Every addiction has its own particular effect on the body and mind. In the next chapter, there is a brief discussion of the more common types of drugs and their physical effects. Here we are interested in the general wear and tear associated with all addictions. The skin can lose its lustre; spots and rashes become more common. The eyes seem sunken and dead, and this deathly appearance is exacerbated by weight loss on the one hand, or a bloated appearance on the other.

The person can experience chronic fatigue and listlessness, alternated with nervous agitation. Speech becomes monotonous and loses its animation. Gestures can slow down, and there is a general feeling that the individual is functioning in a lower gear than normal. The person becomes run-down, often stops eating properly and begins to show signs of physical deterioration. Personal hygiene can also be affected. Less attention is paid to physical appearance and to cleanliness. These are common signs — but there are exceptions to every rule.

Recurrent Illness

Because the addict's physical health is being compromised, he becomes more prone to illness. These illnesses are secondary effects, meaning that they are not caused directly by a particular substance. Infections cause respiratory problems, aches and pains are diagnosed as flu or the common cold. Stomach problems are often seen as food allergies or gastro-enteritis, heart problems are identified and blood pressure is treated. Many of these are called surrogate diagnoses, meaning that they are masking the addiction that causes them. It is estimated that in the United States the treatment for illness caused indirectly by alcohol abuse alone runs to the sum of 50 billion dollars per year. And that is just one drug.

Other symptoms are directly related to the drug used. Flu-like symptoms can result from withdrawal effects. Digestive problems, including gastritis and pancreatitis, are particularly associated with alcohol abuse. Persistent coughing occurs in those who smoke or snort their drugs. The list of possible physical illnesses is too long to present here. When illness seems to be recurring along with some of the other symptoms described above, then one must consider the possibility that some chemical substance is being used.

Summary

This short chapter examined some of the common external signs of addiction. It includes the emotional deterioration, as well as visible changes in the health and appearance of the individual. More specific information on the impact of a variety of different types of addictions is presented below.

CHAPTER 5

Chemical Dependence

Introduction

This chapter examines some of the most common forms of
addiction to mood altering substances. The descriptions
are rather brief, but, in my opinion, give sufficient information
to understand the basic characteristics of each addiction.
The substances described here all have chemical compositions
that affect brain functioning. Thus, it is important to explain
briefly some rudimentary elements of how the brain is affected
by them.

Firstly, it is more accurate to think of the brain not as one
single unit, but as a combination of 'mini brains'. At the top of
the spinal chord, where the nerve cells multiply and broaden
out, we have the basic, simple brain that we share with primitive creatures, such as frogs and fish. This mini-brain looks after
the essential elements of staying alive — breathing, respiration,
circulation, sensory experience and automatic survival skills. It
is the only part that is fully operating in the new-born infant.

Another, more complex, formation covers this simple
structure; we share this with more highly developed creatures,
such as cats, dogs and horses. This mini-brain contains what is
called the limbic system, and looks after physical movement
and instinctual emotional responses. Powerful emotional reactions, including rage, fear and sexual desire are controlled by
this part of the brain.

On top of this mini-brain is the most highly developed
mini-brain, the cerebral cortex. This part provides human

beings with the capacity to think, to create, to choose, to use language and, in general, to experience very high levels of complex functioning. Very undeveloped at birth, the cerebral cortex continues to grow and develop throughout childhood.

The impact of different chemicals is related to the way in which they affect different parts of the brain. A drug that primarily affects the limbic system will, for example, affect the emotions, whereas one that affects the cerebral cortex will influence the ability to think. Many drugs affect more than one part of the brain, and thus can have a generalised effect on thinking and feeling, as well as on basic bodily functioning.

The picture described above is simplistic, and concerns the location of areas of the brain that can be affected by chemicals. It does not reflect the incredibly complex nature of the brain. The vast network of interconnections between the different parts, and the almost infinite numbers of connections within each part, as well as the variety of brain functions, would take a complete book to describe. Here we are limited to a general and simplified picture. One question is, where do chemicals have their impact? Equally important is, how do they do so? The answer to this second question lies in the way that brain cells communicate with each other.

Every human feeling, thought or action involves millions of nerve cells communicating with each other. They do this through the use of complex chemical messengers, called neurotransmitters. Mood-altering drugs have their impact by affecting these chemicals and thus, in turn, influence the communication between brain cells. Different neurotransmitters are responsible for different areas and functions in the brain.

In the discussion below, addictive chemicals will be discussed in terms of the neurotransmitter that they are most likely to affect, thus explaining to some extent the results of taking them. These effects do not suggest that addiction is simply a physical problem. The previous chapter has outlined some of the major psychological elements in addiction, and also that, in certain addictions, these psychological forces are powerful enough to affect brain chemistry directly without the use of a chemical. Let us now turn to some of the most common addictive chemicals.

Alcohol

Ethanol is a colourless, odourless and tasteless chemical, that is the active ingredient in all alcoholic drink. It is a by-product of the chemical reaction involved in the fermentation of sugar and yeast. This active ingredient is a powerful depressant drug. A depressant drug is one which retards or suppresses the functions of the brain and spinal chord (not to be confused with a drug that makes you feel depressed). Depressing the brain functions begins with what are called the higher order functions, namely thinking, perception, control, etc. Lower order brain functions are those regulated by the deeper parts of the brain, and control bodily functions, including breathing and consciousness. The greater the level of alcohol consumed, the more widespread the suppression of brain activity.

A little alcohol makes most people more talkative, less inhibited and often more elated. There is a more devil-may-care attitude, and an ability to take some risks, like chatting with someone you might otherwise feel shy with. Such effects occur because the normal inhibitions and controls used in everyday life are being dismantled. These changes are at work in the recreational use of alcohol, and as such are often quite useful and enjoyable.

Larger amounts of alcohol further decrease control, leading to slurring of speech and lack of co-ordination. Strongly held controls, such as social taboos and moral values, are also diminished. This sometimes leads to inappropriate behaviour, such as pinching someone's bottom in public. Control over the aggressive instinct also diminishes, leading, for example, to a fight with the partner insulted by the bottom pincher! An interesting phenomenon begins to occur when substantial levels of alcohol are involved. The drinker begins to lose two aspects of control: his control of himself socially, morally and physically; as well as (and here is the irony) his ability to judge just how much control he has lost.

To illustrate this further, let us take the familiar scenario of a wedding celebration. During the celebration, it is common for several people to get drunk, often in an inoffensive and playful manner. It is also common for people to be asked to sing. The situation that generally emerges is a good example of what happens when people lose control as well as judgment. The drunken singer launches into a well-known ballad; intense passion is aroused within him, as he bellows out the song completely out of tune, with no rhythm and getting the words wrong.

Those being inflicted with this experience (i.e. those who aren't sufficiently inebriated not to notice) might ask if the singer could possibly not know just how bad it sounds. And, of course, he does not. The alcohol which make the singing so awful has also destroyed the singer's realisation of the situation. This innocuous example illustrates clearly the seductive forces at play in the effect of alcohol on the human being; the very capacities needed to evaluate one's inability to function, and redress the situation, are diminished.

The darker implication of these effects occurs in instances when people overestimate their capacity to drive safely, and then kill someone on the road. I recently heard a story whereby a heavy drinker boasted that he used to drive home when he knew he was unable to walk. His judgment was so impaired that he believed he could manage driving more effectively than walking!

Some statistics from the UK make clear the hugely destructive aspect inherent in the use of alcohol. The *British Medical Journal* reports that alcohol is associated with eighty per cent of deaths from fire, sixty-five per cent of serious head injuries, fifty per cent of murders, forty per cent of road traffic accidents, thirty per cent of fatal accidents, thirty-five per cent of marital breakdowns, and one in three incidents of child abuse. These statistics help to clarify that any drug which diminishes control can also unleash many of the barbaric and destructive elements in the human being.

As more alcohol is consumed, the most primitive functions of the brain are eventually disabled, leading to coma and death. There are, then, three broad levels of effect from the drug: a light dis-inhibiting effect, which functions as a social lubricant; a deeper level of disability, where control and judgment are impaired; and then gross disability, where alcohol poisoning occurs that can lead to death.

Alcohol Addiction

People who become addicted to the drug ethanol are called alcoholics, and they are considered to be suffering from a condition called alcoholism. There are several reasons why these labels are widely used, and there is some argument for changing our way of understanding this problem of alcoholism. These issues are discussed in the section on recovery. Here I will use these labels for the sake of clarity.

Alcoholism is a serious, life-threatening condition, that not only destroys the fabric of an alcoholic's life, but also creates enormous problems for those close to him. This is particularly true for the spouse and children, whose lives are often indelibly marked by the effects of the long-term relationship with the alcoholic.

The condition can be described as one whereby a person continues to drink alcohol, in spite of the obvious damage that it is doing to him, both physically and mentally. The condition has several features, which can best be described as three distinct stages: the adaptive (or early) stage; the dependent (or crucial) stage; and the deteriorative (or chronic) stage.

The adaptive stage of alcoholism is hard to differentiate from normal drinking, in terms of amounts and regularity. Many young people, for example, drink to excess as part of experimentation and rebellion, and are not in this stage of alcoholism. The markers for this stage lie not so much in the drinking habits, but in the relationship the person begins to have with drink.

Some typical characteristics are: using alcohol to feel good, and a growing sense of loss or lack of enjoyment if it is unavailable; developing consistent patterns of drinking that are integrated into life patterns, whilst reducing activities where drink is absent; becoming defensive, or argumentative, if questioned about drinking (implying a growing sense of defensiveness); developing a tolerance for alcohol, i.e. needing to drink more and faster to get the desired effect. The person associates mainly with other drinkers, and chooses relationships with people who tolerate, or actively encourage, drinking. These could be other problem drinkers, or those who are prepared to tolerate excess and unreliability. This stage for most people occurs in the late teenage years into early adulthood.

The dependent stage is characterised by a change from using drink to enhance mood, or increase enjoyment, to its use as a means of reducing anxiety and preventing withdrawal symptoms. It is now being used more directly as a drug fix, although the individual may not recognise this. The amount and frequency increases, and the person begins to show signs of loss of control. He will now drink at times and in places that are inappropriate, such as early morning, during work, at home alone, as well as becoming very anxious about having a supply available.

Personality changes being to occur — care for others decreases, moodiness and preoccupation with self increase. The person becomes less emotionally available, which generally leads to communication breakdown. Physical disorders may occur, including sleeplessness, nausea and tremor. These are usually explained away, or used as a further excuse to drink (i.e. to calm the nerves). Deliberate attempts are made to hide the level of drinking, to explain it away, or to blame others. At this stage, the person is physically and psychologically dependent on alcohol. This stage can last between five and fifteen years.

The deteriorative stage is marked out by serious personality problems, which can include extreme mood swings, outbursts of rage, suicidal depression and increasing isolation. Practical problems reach crisis proportions, financial difficulties emerge, problems at work may mean a threatened job loss. Personal relationships also founder, and complete breakdown in marriage and family relationships can occur. Physical deterioration continues, with digestive disorders, bloated appearance, liver damage (which can become terminal), loss of memory as the brain is distorted, and a host of other physical problems appear.

These can sometimes be presented in isolation for medical help, without any connection being made to the drink problem that causes them. It is considered that up to thirty per cent of hospital beds are taken up by people who are unrecognised and untreated alcoholics. Unless the person gets treatment that directly deals with his drinking, it is likely that death from disease, accident or suicide will result.

A person with a drink problem could read the above description and use the information to convince himself and others that his drinking is not a problem. All he has to do is pick any one symptom described above, and say, 'There, I told you I couldn't be an alcoholic, because I don't suffer from sleepless-ness, financial problems, mood swings etc.' This illustrates the difficulty in describing symptoms and behaviours associated with alcohol abuse. The picture above is a general one, which covers the more common expressions of alcohol addiction.

There are binge drinkers who break out once a month who are addicts; there are those who quietly drink themselves into a comatose state and do not argue or fight, who are also addicted. No matter what way it is expressed in the life of any individual, the addiction is the failure to stop using alcohol, even when great damage is being done as a direct result of drinking. Sometimes the addict is the last person to see his addiction, and will continue in denial for as long as he can, sometimes ably assisted by those around him.

Nicotine

Nicotine is the active ingredient in tobacco, and is ingested by smoking or chewing (less popular now than in the past). Nicotine is a powerfully toxic stimulant drug. It is so toxic that two or three drops of pure nicotine injected into a horse will kill it. Nicotine increases the level of dopamine, a key neurotransmitter, in the emotional centre (limbic system) of the brain, and thus affects mood. A neurotransmitter is a naturally occurring chemical, produced by the body with the express purpose of helping the brain to function.

Most people get their nicotine fix by smoking cigarettes, and in doing so also ingest hundreds of other damaging chemicals, of which carbon monoxide and tar are the most toxic. These toxins add to the physical damage that occurs. All of the nicotine, ninety per cent of the carbon monoxide and seventy per cent of the tar stays in the lungs during the smoking of a cigarette.

Most people start smoking during their teenage years, often as an attempt to cultivate an image of coolness, or rebelliousness. Despite all the warnings (or maybe because of them) few teenagers are truly aware of the dangers that they face in beginning to smoke. Until very recently, cigarette companies denied that cigarette smoking was addictive and harmful. Rather, they promoted their killer products with abandon. Advertising was predominantly concerned with image associations. Some brands were connected to the free spirit and the wide open frontier. Others suggested cool elegance. Still others connected their brand to affluent success. Often in response to these suggestions, and peer group pressure, people start smoking as teenagers and soon become addicted.

Nicotine Addiction

Nicotine is a stimulant that affects mood, decreases appetite, and can facilitate learning and memory. It is legal, widely promoted and lethal. Studies in the United States show that cigarette smoking kills more people than the combined total of those who die from AIDS, cocaine, heroin, alcohol, fire, car accidents, murder and suicide.

Cigarette smoking is perhaps the most dangerous and costly of all addictions. Its seduction lies in the fact that it does not cause immediate injury, but rather does devastating damage over a long period. The health bills facing the economy and the individual are enormous. Treatment for heart and lung diseases (caused by chronic low-level starvation of oxygen to all the major organs), as well as a host of cancers directly related to the toxic effects of nicotine and the other chemicals, soaks up huge financial resources. There is also the direct cost of sustaining the addiction. The average smoker will spend £30,000 to £40,000 on cigarettes alone during his shortened life, money that could go a long way to provide far more life-enhancing activities. You might well ask, why do people do this to themselves? One answer lies in the nature of this form of addiction.

Any drug that is administered by smoking is more likely to impact quickly and intensely on the user. The speed at which it reaches the brain centres where it works makes it potentially more addictive. Nicotine also builds tolerance and creates withdrawal symptoms. This means that there is a gradual increase in the number of cigarettes needed in order to satisfy the smoker's craving. An interesting phenomenon in this regard occurs when a smoker absent-mindedly lights a second cigarette before having finished the first one. Most people who smoke begin to experience withdrawal pangs within thirty minutes of finishing a cigarette. These can be very mild, but increase in intensity if not satisfied, leading to the stereotypical coffee and cigarette first thing in the morning syndrome. All of these characteristics relate to the physical aspects of nicotine addiction, but psychological aspects also play an important role.

The ease with which nicotine can be accessed and used, and the plethora of situations that it is associated with, make it psychologically more addictive. This combination of physical effect and psychological dependence make it extremely difficult to break the hold of nicotine addiction. One study of polydrug users (those who use more than one type of drug) showed that nicotine was rated above heroin, methadone, amphetamine, barbiturates, LSD, marijuana, alcohol and caffeine as the drug they could least do without. You only have to visit a convention of Alcoholics Anonymous to see hundreds of recovering alcohol addicts (many who have been to hell and back to gain sobriety) puffing away on the other very commonly used drug, nicotine.

Prescription and Over-the-Counter Drugs

Prescription drugs are those that are given as a medical intervention, and for the most part are a useful, and sometimes essential, part of treatment for a variety of conditions. Morphine, for example, is a highly addictive pain-killing drug that plays an essential role in treating the pain associated with post-operative recovery, as well as terminal illness. Over-the-counter drugs (aspirin, for example) are those that are used to medicate certain conditions, but do not need a prescription and are therefore not controlled. In this section, I will examine only those prescription drugs that are most often associated with addiction and most open to abuse.

Minor Tranquillisers

Of all prescription medication, the minor tranquillisers are the most open to abuse, and the most likely to lead a user into addiction. This group of drugs is called 'minor', in order to distinguish them from medication used to treat very serious, psychotic conditions. The label 'minor' should not be interpreted to mean safe, or benign.

The most widely used tranquillisers are called benzodiazepines. In general, there are two forms: those that are used primarily to help ease the symptoms of anxiety and nervousness, and those that are used to help an individual to sleep. In the former category, brands such as Valium, Librium, Xanax and Ativan are some of the most common; in the latter, the names Mogodon, Halcion, Dalmane and Royhypnol are well known. There are dozens of different brands on the market, all having the same basic effects.

These drugs act primarily on the central nervous system, and in many ways mimic the effect of alcohol. More specifically, they act by increasing the presence of a neurotransmitter called gamma-aminobutric acid, or GABA for short. This neurotransmitter is found in large quantities in various parts of the brain, and has the effect of slowing down the communication between brain cells. Thus, by increasing the presence of this neurotransmitter, tranquillisers slow down the individual's reactivity and experience, both emotionally and intellectually.

Anxiety is a painful state of fearful vigilance, and any medication that slows down the system will also reduce these symptoms, leaving the individual more relaxed. Tranquillisers are, however, non-specific, insofar as they do not simply act on anxiety — they slow down the whole system. Someone under the influence of tranquillisers may appear slightly drunk, slurring words, lacking in co-ordination, and generally unfocused. Another, less common, group of anti-anxiety medication is called beta-blockers. These drugs are used primarily to deal with heart problems; they are used sometimes for anxiety, because they act on the second-order symptoms of anxiety, namely heart rate and palpitations. These drugs are less addictive.

Tranquilliser Addiction

Any medication or activity that reduces anxiety is potentially addictive. This is because anxiety is one of the most prevalent forms of mental suffering in the developed world, and most people are engaged — to a greater or lesser extent — in reducing, or avoiding, it. Jogging, health clubs, television, counselling, eating and a plethora of other activities are used by many to this end. Tranquillisers are, however, particularly dangerous, because they build tolerance and create withdrawal symptoms.

Tolerance occurs with these drugs because, as with many other substances, the brain adapts to them and limits their impact, which means that the individual must take greater quantities in order to produce the same effect. And the withdrawal effects are particularly severe, because they are used to avoid anxiety. When the drug is removed, the anxiety is still there, but there is now an additional problem. The activity level of the central nervous system increases when the drug is withdrawn, so the person is more sensitive to the fears and worries that still exist. Additionally, they now have to fear their fear, and wonder if they are going to go mad. For some people, addiction to tranquillisers is a nightmare.

Serious questions need to be asked about the use of chemicals to deal with anxiety, given that it seems to be such an endemic part of modern life. Anxiety is, in most cases, circumstantial and environmental and thus is not something that should be 'medicated'. When the minor tranquillisers became widely available, they were immediately successful, and in some cases responsible for a form of long-term, harrowing suffering by those who used them as a short cut to emotional healing.

The Rolling Stones' song 'Mother's Little Helper' called attention to the widespread use of this type of medication, among women in particular, during the 1960s and 1970s.

Because of the current awareness that these drugs are dangerous, they are now prescribed more cautiously, but a great deal of damage has been done. There is also a serious danger of cross addiction with alcohol. It is very easy to see how a person, prescribed these drugs for anxiety, can move to alcohol to escalate the sedating effects, or to replace the pills when the tranquillisers run out. This cocktail of tranquillisers and alcohol is a lethal mix, and can lead to death from overdose.

Many years ago, I read a most vivid and illuminating story of the nature of tranquilliser addiction in the book *I'm Dancing as Fast as I Can*. This true story reflects the gradual take-over and loss of control of the individual addicted to tranquillisers. In general, life becomes a journey marked out between pills. As worry and fearfulness make themselves felt, the individual takes a pill. Within a short period, there is a calming feeling of relaxation that gradually wears off, requiring another pill.

Then there is the fear of the supply running out. The panic of finding oneself in a shopping centre and realising that the pills are at home leads to vertigo, dizziness and shortness of breath, as the fear begins to rise like a wave ready to overwhelm the tranquilliser addict. Night-time pills are needed to sleep, morning pills to help meet the day, lunch-time pills to help cope with the nervous feelings, tea-time pills to cope with coming home, or the spouse returning. On and on it goes, as the individual becomes completely lost in a fog of chemical sedation.

Amphetamines

Amphetamines are a group of drugs that were originally designed for useful medical purposes. They were synthesised after it was discovered that ephedrine was the active ingredient in an ancient Chinese herbal treatment for asthma.

Amphetamine was the closest chemical equivalent to ephedrine, and was very successful with asthma because it had a profound effect on the level of adrenaline in the body. Later, these drugs were used as appetite suppressants (slimming pills), and they were also used to treat mild depression. All of these effects were noted in the approval given by the American Food and Drug Administration (FDA) for their use as prescription medication.

Currently, amphetamines have a much reduced usage, and are far more likely to be found on sale on the black market. They are often referred to as the poor man's cocaine (they have remarkably similar effects). A particularly dangerous and innovative form is that of the amphetamine derivative Methylamphetamine hydrochloride, with the name ice, or crystal meth, because of its transparent sheet-like crystals. It vaporises easily and can be smoked, leading to a powerful high. A near relative to amphetamine is one of the active ingredients in the drug Ecstasy.

Amphetamine is now recognised as extremely addictive, and dangerous. Consequently, its medical use is very restricted. It is mainly prescribed in the form of the drug Ritalin, which is used to treat the rather controversial condition called attention deficit disorder (ADD) in children. It is also used to treat the less common sleep disorder called narcolepsy.

Amphetamines gained prominence and infamy in the halcyon years of the drug culture, the 1960s. They were embraced and idealised by those who used them as a stand-alone fix that gave constant highs and extreme euphoria. This group of junkies was eventually given a class of its own within the drug culture — speed freaks. Others used the brands Benzedrine (bennies), Dexedrine, Quaaludes (ludes) to accentuate the altered states produced by LSD. The attraction of amphetamines to the drug-hungry sub-culture led to government concern and a crackdown on availability.

Amphetamine Addiction

Amphetamines are powerful stimulant drugs, which work by boosting the activity of the neurotransmitters dopamine, nor-epinephrine and serotonin. This global effect means that they increase the level of activity in both the emotional and intel-lectual centres of the brain. Amphetamines were used regularly by the armed forces in both the Second World War and in Vietnam. They allowed people to go beyond normal endurance, both physically and mentally. Others, particularly university students, used them to help cram for exams. The heightened awareness and concentration levels produced by the drugs' effects on the cerebral cortex meant that people could study for nights without sleep, and still have the energy to arrive in time for the exam. Much disillusion followed, however, when they discovered that they could not recall what they had learned.

Amphetamines produce serious psychological addiction, as well as carrying potential for massive emotional breakdown. One of the intriguing effects of heavy use is the phenomenon of amphetamine psychosis. This occurs when the individual shows the signs and symptoms of serious mental illness, namely schizo-phrenia. In most cases, the heavy user becomes increasingly paranoid and confused. Many murders have been committed by those in a full-blown, amphetamine-produced paranoid state. This phenomenon was so widespread in the United States that it gave new meaning to the phrase 'speed kills'.

Another major effect of heavy amphetamine use is what became termed 'the crash'. This is a state of complete exhaustion and emotional depression, which occurs in the after-math of the amphetamine high. There is a commonly accepted rule in psychopharmacology that 'what goes up must come down'. Many heavy users cannot bear the withdrawal effects, and take opiates such as heroin, or tranquillisers, to ease the pain of the crash. This leads to cross addiction, and a very poor prognosis for a drug-free life.

Anti-Depressants

Another group of prescription drugs that has some potential for addiction is anti-depressants. It is commonly believed among the medical profession that these drugs are not addictive, a belief based on several assumptions. These drugs do not produce tolerance, that is, the user does not need to increase the dosage when taking them over a long period. Thus, they do not fulfil one of the important criteria for addiction. Secondly, in the initial stage of usage, they do not provide an immediate chemical effect that alters mood. Consequently, they are not attractive to an addictive drug user and have little sales value on the black market. Therefore, they do not have a high abuse potential. The people who are addicted to anti-depressants are likely to be under medical care, and to be taking their medication responsibly for 'depressive illness'. They will not, in general, know that they are addicted until they try to stop the medication.

There are three different types of anti-depressant medication: tricyclics, SSRIs (Selective Serotonin Reuptake Inhibitors) and MAOIs (Monoamine Oxidase Inhibitors). In terms of addictive potential, we are only interested in the first two because of the way they act on the brain. MAOIs are more likely to be used when a person has not responded to either of the other types. MAOIs are prescribed cautiously, because they are extremely toxic, and if taken with certain foods or other medicine (e.g. certain types of cough linctus) they can lead to massive cardiovascular crisis, or stroke.

Tryciclic anti-depressants have a long history, but are now being replaced with a new generation drug (the SSRIs). Tricyclics were originally developed as a treatment for schizophrenia, and have their impact by boosting the availability of the neurotransmitters norepinephrine and serotonin. For most of their history, it was considered that their impact on norepinephrine was most active in relieving depression. It also led to the side effects of nausea, dizziness, dry mouth, etc. The chemical effect of tricyclics was somewhat similar to that of amphetamines, but did not create the same experience in the user. This may be because amphetamines both increase the amount as well as maintain the level of norepinephrine, whereas the tricyclics do not actually add to the levels.

As theories of depression developed, one line of inquiry suggested that these drugs were having their impact on depression by affecting the neurotransmitter serotonin, and that perhaps a drug that acted on serotonin alone would be most effective.

This research led to the new generation of SSRIs and the household name Prozac. Prozac and its near relatives, Seroxat and Lustrol, are now the most widely prescribed antidepressants, as well as becoming a cultural phenomenon in the United States. Many people, who are not clinically depressed, are taking these drugs to boost morale and energy levels. Like the amphetamine craze of the 1960s, we are seeing a medical treatment losing its clinical moorings and being brought into the consumer market simply to make people feel happier.

Addiction to Anti-Depressants

We have seen above that these drugs do not produce tolerance, and are therefore, strictly speaking, not addictive. They are, however, very potent, and do produce chemical dependency. Serotonin is one of the more important neurotransmitters related to mood. The part of the brain that is crucial to pleasure, appetite and sleep regulation (the hypothalamus) is almost completely constructed of serotonin-based nerve cells. By increasing the availability of serotonin in this area of the brain, the user's mood, appetite and sleep patterns are affected.

Serotonin also plays a more widespread role in other areas of the brain. Long-term use of anti-depressants may lead to a compensation in the brain for the presence of greater levels of serotonin. The brain may react by lowering the production of serotonin, which can then cause painful withdrawal effects. When the drug is withdrawn, the person may experience deeper depression than before. This is often taken as proof that the medication is treating their depressive illness. There is, however, an alternative explanation.

By lowering the brain's sensitivity to serotonin, the very substance that is supposed to help people feel better, results in their feeling worse. It is my experience that some people getting off this kind of medication can experience harrowing emotional turmoil. Mood swings, a feeling of becoming over-whelmed, dizziness and a general feeling of physical malaise all seem to be regular features of withdrawal. It is irresponsible for any practitioner to prescribe these drugs without informing the patient that he may find it difficult to stop taking them.

The Opiates

This group of drugs is so named because the drugs are derivatives of opium. The most common synthetic variations in medical usage are morphine, codeine and methadone, and they are used primarily as pain relievers. It is well known that recovery from surgery is badly affected if a patient experiences constant pain, and in some situations the minor pain-relieving drugs are not strong enough to give relief. It is in these situations, and with the terminally ill, that morphine is used. Codeine is a milder form of opiate, but once taken it is converted to morphine by the body. The powerfully addictive nature of these drugs has led to a far more cautious control on their distribution and usage. Until the turn of the century, it was possible to buy morphine over the counter at the local apothecary.

Chemically, the opiates work by mimicking the naturally occurring pain-relieving substances in the brain. These are called endorphins, which are involved in both pain relief and pleasure. Sexual intercourse and physical exercise, such as jogging, for example, lead to a release of endorphins that are experienced as feelings of pleasure. Injury also leads to a release of endorphins, resulting in the relief of pain. Opiates share some similarities with tranquillisers, in their tendency to make the user feel drowsy and serene, but their most powerful seduction is in the tremendous rush of warm well-being that they produce. It is this effect that has led to their attraction and usage in an addictive manner.

I will discuss addiction to opiates in the section on illegal drugs, because heroin is the primary opiate of abuse, and yet it shares most of the characteristics of those drugs used in conventional medicine.

Illegal Drugs

Thus far, we have discussed the addictions that account for the greatest damage to human beings. The negative impact on society and on human life from the use of illegal drugs is minuscule in comparison to the damage from those that are available legally. The effects of illegal drug-taking are somewhat more sensational, and thus seem to make a greater impact. When a young person dies after taking one Ecstasy tablet, there is a major outcry and much media interest. Whilst each such incident is a terrible tragedy in its own right, it is matched by several hundred people dying from alcohol- or nicotine-related illness. Every week, newspapers carry sensational accounts related to drug addiction. This week's example reads, 'Drug carnage like a war — every stratum of society is taking causalities'. When was the last time a newspaper gave headline attention to an ordinary person — as distinct from a celebrity — dying from liver failure due to alcohol abuse? Or from emphysema due to cigarette smoking?

A great deal of the damage associated with the use of illegal substances is a direct result of the fact that their usage has been criminalised. Let us take a simple example. Heroin is a very powerful drug. A huge amount of violence is associated with its use. People are attacked by addicts who are strung out and desperate for money to buy a fix. Gangland drug lords kill each other, or anyone who gets in their way, for access to the incredibly profitable black market. These effects have nothing to do with the *actual* effect of heroin on the addict. Heroin does not make people violent — in fact it has the opposite effect, causing drowsiness, apathy and euphoria. The drug that is most likely to lead to violence in its direct chemical effect is — you guessed it — alcohol.

This point is important in any rational discussion of the use of illegal drugs. We must try to separate the effects of the drug itself on the individual from the effects of carrying out criminal activity in order to gain access to it: these are two different issues. With regard to addiction, our concern is with the first area. The second area belongs in the arena of legal and political strategies used to control the availability of certain substances, and is beyond the scope of this book.

Hallucinogenic Drugs

This group of drugs is so named because they affect a person's perception of reality. Whilst some of the drugs discussed above can carry hallucinatory effects, none of them are specifically taken for this reason. Hallucinogens are those drugs that are specifically used for their impact on perception. Their common feature is to dis-inhibit the control of the normal waking mind, and to lead the user into a different state of consciousness, where there is often a flooding awareness of colour and light, a feeling of oceanic unity, and a very heightened sensory awareness.

Philosopher and educationalist William James describes the effects of these drugs thus:

> One conclusion was forced upon my mind, and
> my impression of its truth has ever since remained
> unshaken. It is that our normal waking consciousness,

rational consciousness as we call it, is but one special type of consciousness, whilst all about it, parted from it by the flimsiest of screens, there lie potential forms of consciousness entirely different. We may go through life without suspecting their existence; but apply the requisite stimulus, and at a touch they are there in all their completeness ... No account of the universe in its totality can be final which leaves these other forms of consciousness quite disregarded.

Thus, a century ago, we see an eminent scholar naming the significance of hallucinogens to our understanding of human consciousness. Since that time, and particularly during the experimental years of the 1960s, the use of hallucinogens has become widespread.

Much of the specific effect of hallucinogens on the chemistry of the brain remains a mystery. They do seem to have the effect of selectively reducing the impact of external stimuli by blocking certain neurotransmitters, whilst increasing the brain's sensitivity to internal, and often subconscious, data. In a way, it is inaccurate to call these drugs hallucinogenic, because they do not create any new information or mental events. Rather, they increase the user's attention to, and focus on, experiences that already exist. Recent research suggests that the active ingredient in much of the chemical effects is a naturally occurring brain substance called tryptamine, which is released by the pineal gland.

A more recent argument regarding the power of these drugs is that whilst they do not produce new mental events, neither do they rely totally on internal sensations. Rather, they attune the mind to become accessible to a different reality, one that is just as important and 'real' as the events noticed in the ordinary levels of consciousness. Thus, many of the events that occur under the influence of hallucinogenic drugs belong to the spiritual and esoteric plane of human consciousness.

An interesting analogy may clarify this viewpoint. The rather crude comparison of the human brain with a radio receiver allows us to consider the way the brain might be receptive to certain kinds of signals. Tuning a radio to a certain frequency allows us access to certain channels, and, equally, denies us access to others. Perhaps different forms of consciousness are like the radio tuner — they open the mind to the voices and signals of a certain reality, whilst closing accessibility to others.

In normal waking consciousness, our brains are tuned to the channel of what can be experienced through the senses, and processed by the intellectual programme that exists in our minds as a result of learning. It is argued by many that this area of experience is only one of a number of different realities that can be experienced, each requiring a different form of consciousness.

Everybody experiences the obviously different forms of consciousness involved in dreaming whilst asleep on the one hand, and waking consciousness on the other. Perhaps there are other forms of consciousness, ones that can be encountered through various types of meditation, ritual practices and drugs. Much of the evidence from a variety of different cultures, as well as from certain areas of psychotherapy, suggests this to be the case. The question that remains is whether the voices, visions and messages delivered to the individual in altered states of consciousness have an objective though secret reality, or are they simply the product of overactive imaginations stimulated by the juices of the brain? It is beyond the scope of this book to examine this fundamentally important question.

Addiction to Hallucinogens

The more common hallucinogens are marijuana, LSD, DMT, mescaline, psilocybin (either synthetic, or in the form of magic mushrooms) and some forms of MDMA (Ecstasy). There is little evidence to suggest that these drugs are physically addictive.

Although marijuana is in a class of its own (i.e. cannabinoids), I have included it here because it is mildly hallucinogenic. It is by far the most commonly used illegal substance, and is smoked in some form or other (hashish or grass) as a recreational drug by hundreds of millions worldwide. Most of the evidence available suggests that it is less toxic than either cigarette smoke or alcohol. Thus, there is much argument in favour of its decriminalisation.

Marijuana is psychologically addictive. Its capacity to assist people to tune out of reality, to escape the pressures of life, and to provide a serene and calm experience, all go to make its use seductive and attractive. Many people seem to be able to use this drug now and then as part of an occasion or celebration, with little or no long-term impact or side effects. Others, however, become what are called 'heads', consistently stoned, apathetic, lacking in concentration, and somewhat paranoid. It is my experience that this level of use can ruin a person's life.

LSD, DMT and mescaline are far more powerful hallucinogens. These drugs are the synthetic equivalents of natural hallucinogenic substances found in a variety of plants and fungi, including the desert root-plant peyote, and the vine banisteriopsis. These plants and others like them have been used for many centuries as part of the rituals of a variety of cultures, including the native American Indian. They are usually considered sacred, and are used carefully within the cultural taboos of the appropriate tribe or group. The synthetic equivalents are, however, not given the same respect, nor have they the same purpose. They, like marijuana, are not physically addictive. They do however, build tolerance, and cross tolerance; this means that if the drug of choice is LSD, then the user will have to use more and more to get an effect, and he will have to use larger amounts of the others — such as mescaline — if he changes over to them.

These drugs are psychologically addictive and, in my opinion, extremely dangerous. This does not mean that they have no value. Their history within certain cultures, and the interest that is taken in them as therapeutic agents in a clinical setting, suggests that they may have some value for emotional healing and spiritual growth. In the vast majority of cases, these drugs are used to tune out of conscious reality and to provide an electrifying sensory overload, which it is hoped will be positive and enjoyable.

Crucial to the careful use of these drugs are two important considerations, namely the setting and the set. The setting refers to the environment in which the drugs are taken; the set refers to the mind-set of the user at the time of experiment-ation. Most people who use them do not know the importance of these elements, and are playing Russian roulette with their psychological integrity. Insanity is a real risk for those who carry psychological vulnerability and a fragile identity within their psychological make-up, and who try to journey beyond the grey zone of their lives by using these drugs. Stable, mature indi-viduals have less to fear. Then again, do we really know ourselves and the demons that often lurk in the unconscious well enough to tempt them, with such elixirs, into conscious awareness and experience?

The Opiates

We have examined the basic effects of opiate drugs in the discussion of prescription drugs above. Here we are mainly concerned with the most well-known, and infamous, drug — heroin. There is a certain irony in the name. Heroin comes from the word hero, and was used to label this drug because it was expected to show heroic success in helping people to come off its close relatives, morphine and opium. In 1901, the *New York Medical Journal* wrote, 'Heroin will take the place of morphine, without its disagreeable qualities.' Its use for this purpose is a good example of the cure being worse than the disease. Heroin turned out to be far more potent and addictive than the drugs it was to replace.

Additionally, its use led to many other problems, in addition to that of addiction. Currently, heroin addicts face huge risks from infection due to contaminated needles (by far the greatest cause of the spread of AIDS in this country), as well as toxic side effects due to the chemical mixes used to cut street heroin. Other opiates are morphine, methadone, pethedine and codeine. Certain compounds have been synthesised from these prescription pain-killers, the best known being 'China white', a synthetic version of heroin that is many times stronger than morphine.

Opiate Addiction

Opiates are physically and psychologically addictive. Much like addiction to alcohol, there are recognisable stages in the progression of this type of addiction, whether it is a doctor or pharmacist addicted to pethedine, or an unemployed heroin addict. During the adaptive stage, the drug is used as a means of coping with stress or emotional pain, or to produce a high. This rather quickly leads to tolerance, so that greater amounts are needed and withdrawal symptoms occur when the drug wears off.

The move from the adaptive to the dependent stage occurs much faster than with alcohol — usually within a number of weeks the person becomes physically and emotionally dependent. The dependent stage is marked out by strong craving for the drug, much more intense withdrawal effects, and more difficulty getting high. The focus of drug use now becomes a rather desperate attempt to ward off the intensely painful withdrawal effects. Additionally, the drug becomes the centre of attention, and there is an obsession with availability. Criminal activity increases among those with no ready access to the drug, particularly in the case of heroin, which is, in any case, illegal. Sexual performance deteriorates and other physical problems begin to occur, particularly among those using contaminated needles or impure substances.

The chronic stage leads to complete collapse of moral, intellectual and emotional functioning. There is loss of family, financial ruin, deep depression and strong risks of suicide or death by overdose. Without help at this stage, the person will die or end up in jail as a direct or indirect result of his addiction.

Psychostimulants

This group of drugs includes the amphetamines discussed above. They differ from the opiates and hallucinogens, in that their primary function is to increase the activity level of the central nervous system. Their effect is to heighten energy, speed up reactions and give a high, exciting boost to all the senses. The most common illegal stimulant drugs are cocaine, its synthetic equivalent crack, and MDMA. Better known as Ecstasy, MDMA was originally developed as an appetite suppressant in Germany, in 1914. It is a potent combination of both hallucinogenic and amphetamine chemicals, and is the drug of choice of the rave generation of the 1990s. When combined with rave music, it provides the user with an altered state of consciousness; this is marked out by a massive increase in energy (the amphetamine effect), euphoric feelings of con-nection to others, and oceanic bliss (this effect leading to it being termed the love drug).

The danger of death due to dehydration, heart failure and chemical collapse resulting in coma and death have been high-lighted in the media. These dangers are, however, the extreme end of the spectrum. By putting a sensationalist stress on these extreme effects, users are led to dismiss any negative state-ments about the use of Ecstasy as propaganda by conservative and unenlightened pillars of society. This drug is, however, extremely dangerous, because of its come-down effects and its long-term impact on the chemistry of the brain. Its effect on serotonin levels can lead consistent users into long-term depression. It also leads some users into cross addiction with heroin or other opiates that are used to cope with the crash, the emotional fatigue and burn-out experienced in the aftermath of the high.

Cocaine is a powerful stimulant drug that affects the central nervous system by increasing the levels of dopamine, serotonin and norepinephrine. It has been used for thousands of years by the South American Indians to combat fatigue and hunger. It was ingested by chewing the leaf of the coca bush, which meant a much slower intake and less of a high. It was introduced into Europe in the 1850s for use as a local anaesthetic, and made famous by Sigmund Freud, who prescribed it to a friend as a cure for his morphine addiction, thus creating the first known cocaine addict. Freud himself then became addicted to cocaine.

Currently, it is used medically in what is known as the 'Brompton Cocktail', a combination of cocaine and other pain-killers used to alleviate the suffering of terminally ill cancer patients. Crack is a form of cocaine which is smoked, and gives a faster and more intense hit. This is a particularly hazardous use of the drug, and leads to more deaths from heart attacks, strokes and damage to heart and lungs than does the more conventional form, which involves snorting cocaine powder through the nose.

Cocaine Addiction

As with many other drugs, there is a fiction that cocaine is not physically addictive. This is based on the fact that cocaine does not seem to produce observable physical withdrawal effects. As the body metabolises or breaks down the drug, it does not appear to react to the drug's absence by causing illness, or physical pain. Thus, it is considered not to be addictive. This is, however, questionable, because cocaine use does produce very strong craving as well as great feelings of loss of well-being in some people. It may be that these cravings are in fact physical rather than psychological in origin.

More and more evidence is being accumulated that shows that consistent use of cocaine has a devastating effect on the brain's reactivity to dopamine, one of the key neurotransmitters. If this is the case, then it would appear that by damaging the brain's receptivity to dopamine, the user runs the risk of long-term, chronic depression. This depression is physical in origin, and can be considered a delayed withdrawal reaction to cocaine.

Cocaine addiction tends to progress through three stages. The first stage can be termed the experimental stage, and involves using cocaine to enhance feelings and out of curiosity. There is no major impact on social, emotional or physical functioning. Generally, the individual uses the drug only in situations where it is offered, and perhaps in the company of others. This stage can rather quickly lead on to the compulsive stage.

In the compulsive stage, there is a gradual disruption of the person's life style. The user buys cocaine more regularly, begins to distance from non-users and also makes attempts to change. Mood swings begin to feature and financial problems begin. There is frequent overspending and increased social withdrawal. The user then moves into the dysfunctional stage.

This stage is marked out by a growing inability to function in relationships and work. The user begins to experience chronic sleep and nutritional disorders. Very high doses are used, leading to serious medical problems. The user begins to look sick, and may use other drugs to cope with the growing disorder, the terrible depressions and emotional crashes experienced in the come-down from the fix. There is total preoccupation with the drug, which is now used in order to feel normal and to cope with guilt. Financial ruin can lead to stealing, embezzlement or dealing in drugs to support the habit. There is a growing risk of serious physical damage to heart, lungs and nasal cavity. In one interview, a celebrity talked of his horror when in company he sneezed and the whole tissue of his nasal cavity erupted and hung down his face, to the horror of those around him.

Miscellaneous

Thus far, we have discussed the more commonly used addictive drugs. There is however, a growing market for all kinds of chemically prepared mood-altering substances, and new potions, or combinations are continually being brought into the drug-hungry market. Recent additions are Ketamine (or special K to the user). This drug was widely used in Vietnam as a battlefield anaesthetic. It has also found use as a horse tranquilliser! It is hallucinogenic and produces an extreme relaxed state. Side effects can lead to paralysis and long-term mental problems. GHB, sometimes known as liquid Ecstasy, is also becoming more common, and has the same effects and side effects as its relative discussed above. Amyl nitrate (poppers) used mainly heretofore to increase the intensity of sexual orgasm — particularly among the gay community — is now part of the night-club scene.

Solvents are a particularly dangerous group of chemicals. They are inhaled, and include anti-freeze, paint thinner, correction fluid and glues. Most contain an industrial solvent called Tuolene, which may be the active ingredient. The user gets a dizzy high as the main effect. These chemicals cause serious harm to the lungs and throat, but most particularly cause severe and irreparable brain damage. One highly addictive everyday drug is caffeine, which is a stimulant and leads to quite severe withdrawal symptoms for some who try to cut down on intake.

Summary

This chapter has examined some of the more common forms of substance addiction. One of its central points is that different drugs have different effects on the brain and central nervous system, and thus on the actual experience of the user. I believe that these different effects are central to understanding the meaning of addiction for any particular individual. Furthermore, this aspect needs to be considered in any approach that has as its focus the treatment or prevention of addiction. This will be discussed in more detail in a later chapter. Chemical addictions are the more dramatic forms of addiction. There is however, growing evidence that psychological addictions can be as powerful, and sometimes as destructive, as their chemical counterparts. It is to this issue that we now turn.

CHAPTER 6

Psychological Addiction

Introduction

There is some debate as to the validity of the term addiction to describe activities that do not involve an addictive substance. Some argue that the meaning of addiction is lost if it is used to refer to activities other than drug-taking. I have some sympathy with this viewpoint, but it is becoming clear that we cannot distinguish the biology of addiction from its psychological elements. All addiction involves changing the chemistry of the brain. Drug abuse does it in a more intense and recognisable manner. Recent research shows, however, that certain behaviours also impact on brain function; these are, therefore, addictive even within the biological sense of the word.

It seems more useful to speak of two broad areas of addiction: those that relate to certain chemicals, i.e. chemical addiction; and those that relate to activities, i.e. addictive behaviours. This chapter concerns some of the major psycho-logical addictions.

Compulsive Gambling

For many people, the notion that someone can become addicted to gambling seems unlikely. It seems rather strange that a person can feel tremendous craving and a powerful compulsion to bet on a horse, or spend hours in front of a poker machine. To a clear-thinking person, such behaviour seems rather easy to avoid if one wishes to. Gambling addiction is, however, a much more complex business than simply wanting badly to take betting risks. It is also hugely destructive. The obvious damage that is incurred financially is often reflective of equally destructive emotional, spiritual and intellectual destruction.

The intricate nature of gambling addiction is not well understood, because it has only been recognised as a serious disorder in recent years. It is now the third most commonly treated addiction after alcohol and drugs, and is often termed the drugless addiction. Several elements are now emerging, which tend to be an underlying part of the disorder. Gambling addicts for the most part tend to deal with emotional distress by using defence mechanisms of distraction and rationalisation. In other words, like other types of addicts, they have a lot of problems coping with their feelings.

What tends to set these addicts apart is their use of thinking as a means of avoidance. Once this pattern is established, they are prime candidates for gambling problems. Having tasted the experience of gambling, they have been presented with a situation that can utilise all their mental energy. The risks inherent in betting occupy the mind, and eventually take it over completely. Allied to this is the adrenaline surge that is inherent in the excitement of the risk of winning or losing.

Compulsive gamblers will bet on anything — or more accurately will try to turn everything into an opportunity to gamble. A recent experience usefully illustrates this point. On a visit to London, I was taking a guided tour that included visiting some of the historic clubs associated with the English aristocracy. One of the least useful bits of information given by the guide was the account of a member of the Royal family who bet £3,000 (a vast sum at the time) with a colleague as to which of two raindrops trickling down the window pane would reach the bottom first!

Most gamblers do not indulge in such trivial attempts, but the principle behind their activities is the same. Gradually, a cycle of obsessional thinking about gambling takes a firmer and firmer hold on the person's mind. Tiredness and financial loss lead to taking higher and more impulsive betting risks, with even less chance of success. Emotionally exhausted from the outcome of this addiction, the gambler has fewer and fewer resources to attend to his relationships, his family and his work. Gradually, as financial problems mount, he becomes more and more secretive and deceitful, mortgaging more and more of his resources in the growing difficulties of losing more and more money, all the while hoping for the big win that will relieve him of this burden. Should this win occur, he is likely to lose it all again, and so the cycle continues. This cycle is akin to someone trying to dig themselves out of a hole using a shovel — all they do is get in deeper.

Most untreated gambling addicts eventually lose everything they own — and often a lot of what they don't own — leading to lifelong debt and financial impoverishment. Emotional withdrawal follows, with deeper anxiety sometimes leading to suicide, or turning to some other addictive substance such as alcohol. Over a period of years, the person becomes an emotional and spiritual wreck.

Eating Disorders

Perhaps the best example of addictive behaviour is found among those who suffer from eating disorders. In the main, there are three different types of disorder: compulsive overeating, bulimia and anorexia nervosa. Overeating is the least complex of these disorders. For the most part, the individual craves for food and eats beyond the body's natural requirements, leading to obesity and a variety of physical disorders, usually resulting in early death. Food is largely being used as a mood altering substance — a drug — rather than as a nutritional requirement. This is the key to understanding it as an addiction problem.

Furthermore, certain types of food lend themselves to use as a drug, particularly white sugar, refined flour and chocolate. White sugar gives an instant boost to the energy system, followed by low blood sugar fatigue. The average American consumes forty to forty-five teaspoons of sugar per day! White flour is a dead food that is usually combined with sugar and a host of food additives, all having chemical effects. Chocolate contains phenylalinine, a substance related to mood which is found in small quantities in the brain, as well as theobromine, which has a stimulant effect. These are the most common forms of what have become known as trigger foods. These are foods that, when taken, lead the individual to binge. It is likely that strong effects on the brain chemistry are triggered by the psychological association with the taste and texture, as well as the direct impact on body chemistry.

Evidence suggests that overeating is, in some cases, a result of food allergy; new methods of blood analysis are showing encouraging results in tracking down food sensitivities for some overeaters. The roots of most overeating problems are, however, emotional in origin. We now know that early life experiences have a profound effect on the way that the brain constructs itself, and furthermore that the associations between emotional states and certain experiences are deeply ingrained in the brain pathways.

It is also true to say that one of the earliest associations in infancy is the connection between being fed and the feeling of comfort and safety. For some people, this association appears to continue, for complex reasons, into adult life; this leads them to associate, often unconsciously, the experience of eating with emotional happiness. Because eating does not, in fact, heal emotional pain or solve emotional problems, an individual can find himself in a continual cycle of overeating — relief, emotional distress, further eating, relief, emotional distress, and so on. This cycle is indistinguishable from those involved in other drug addictions.

Bulimia is often considered to be an attempt by an overeater to minimise the physical effect of their disorder by preventing the intake of calories. This disorder is the cycle of bingeing on food and then purging the body by getting sick, using laxatives and excessive exercise. This cycle is extremely damaging to the individual's digestive system, can damage the heart, depletes essential potassium levels, rots teeth and affects skin and hair. It is more likely, however, that bulimia has stronger links to anorexia nervosa than it has to overeating.

Anorexia nervosa, originally called the slimmers' disease, is a dramatically dangerous, addictive behaviour that involves compulsive starvation, obsession with body weight and image, and is fatal in up to twenty per cent of cases. Perhaps few disorders reflect the power of the mind as does this one. At some stage, the person — very often an adolescent girl — begins to focus on body image, and starts to control food. This is, of course, a very common behaviour among adolescents who wish to remain slim, and who have taken on the cultural value that being slim is a necessary part of being attractive.

A certain number of these young people find that, within a short time, their desire to control food has turned into a compulsion, and a nightmare. Losing more and more weight, their perception begins to change and they lose any accurate, or realistic, view of their own bodies. They see fat where there is none, and can look at their emaciated figure in a mirror and see a fat person looking back. Parents and friends of the anorectic individual begin to panic and to try all kinds of pressure to get the person to eat. This generally leads the individual to become manipulative and clever in disguising their starvation. Telling lies, acting out and the plethora of other types of devious behaviour are symptoms of the disorder, rather than any character flaw in the individual.

In many cases, bulimia seems to occur as a symptom of anorexia. Because anorexia is centrally a compulsion to control what is a primal biological imperative, namely eating, a tremendous conflict emerges between the intense reaction of the body to starvation, and the almost religious zeal to prevent food being taken. As the conflict heightens, a craving for food gets stronger; if the individual capitulates — especially with a trigger food, such as a cake, or chocolate bar — a massively overwhelming compulsion may ensue, where the individual eats to the point of exhaustion.

The terror then builds, because the starving body is satisfied and the obsessive mind screams to get rid of the food. Vomiting, panic-stricken exercise and laxatives are all drawn in to flush the body. Eventually, some semblance of peace ensues as control is regained. The body has been further damaged, and the cycle begins to build again. Eventually, the person either recovers in their own time, or gets the help they need to recover; others starve to death.

There is little evidence to suggest that anorexia or bulimia is a biochemical disorder. It is more likely that any biological features are symptoms rather than causes of this syndrome. The vast majority of people who become anorexic are adolescent girls. The incidence rate has increased dramatically in the last two decades, and existing statistics suggest that one per cent of Europeans and Americans will have some encounter with this problem.

Additionally, recent studies confirm that Argentina is fast becoming the anorexic capital of the world, with a rate four times that of the United States. These statistics are strong evidence that there are major cultural influences in the development of this disorder. As with most addictions, the social climate, and the values and taboos of different societies, influence the kinds of addiction that become prevalent.

Shopping

The idea that culture affects the prevalence of certain types of addiction is further supported by the advent of compulsive shopping as an addictive disorder. A recent bumper sticker sums it up nicely in the phrase 'born to shop'. In societies where basic physical needs are met, and profit-making is the central function of business, a whole superstructure is created to encourage and beguile people into buying what they don't really need. This structure includes convincing people that owning certain goods meets psychological needs, such as status, power, attraction to the opposite sex, security and so on.

Most people in modern society are to some extent prey to the illusions wrought upon them through marketing strategies, and most get some comfort and pleasure from accumulating possessions in this manner. For some, however, the experience of shopping becomes compulsive and addictive. In general, as with most addictions, the activity is carried on in order to meet needs that it cannot meet, and is often driven by unconscious motives and emotions.

People who shop addictively tend to obsess on the shopping trip, distracting themselves from difficulties or problems by focusing on the pleasurable feeling they get when they visit the shops. The focus is not on whether the items are needed, or even desired; it is on the act of buying: and it is this act that is central to the disorder. This is why some addicts buy several pairs of the same shoes, or the same clothes, knowing that on reflection they will not use them. The need to buy is the driving force — it doesn't really matter what is bought.

Closer examination of the problem reveals that underlying forces are at work. The person may be seeking to replace an emptiness within, or feels somehow more powerful by virtue of a buying spree. All the attendant experiences of the shopping expedition may also be having a subconscious impact. The feeling of being anonymous in the crowd, or a sense of belonging, or then again simply the attention being paid by the shop assistant, may all be at work. Psychological addiction to shopping is as individual as the person who suffers with it. Long-term recovery, as with most addiction, involves understanding the meaning of the addiction for each individual, and the forces that are particularly at work in each situation.

The Silver Screen

Addiction to television is as old as the apparatus itself. It is marked out by a compulsive need to tune out of everyday reality, and to enter the world of the soap opera, constant replays of the news, and channel surfing. Like most useful and beneficial things, television can become a source of great loss and waste. Television addicts lose the ability to be with themselves, or perhaps more accurately, may never have developed a mature sense of their own identity, as well as a motivation to learn and grow. Perhaps life is just too difficult, and it is easier to live out your existence in the unreal world produced by the media moguls.

We have seen in the discussion of drug addiction that two key elements are tolerance and withdrawal: tolerance meaning a need for more of the substance to get relief or a high, and withdrawal the growth of insecure, anxious and painful feelings, when the substance is not available. Television addicts are people who spend more and more of their waking hours locked into television, and who feel odd and uncomfortable in the silence when it is turned off.

The growth of this kind of addiction has seen the production of magazine publications devoted to the story lines of television series. A person can now read about the transplant that Bill is waiting for and wonder if it will succeed, and if his wife will find out that he has been having an affair with Glenda when she visits him at the hospital. Coffee breaks at work may be spent discussing this issue, all in an amazing acceptance that fictional characters created by scriptwriters have taken on a greater reality in the mind of the addict. Recently, one daily newspaper carried front-page pictures of two people crying in each other's arms. This was the reported break-up of the relationship between these two soap opera characters — it had no bearing on any reality.

Television provides entertainment, recreation and education, and is perhaps one of the great additions to quality of life for many people. It is, however, potentially dangerous for some, who become addicted to it as means of avoiding any constructive approach to living with themselves and others.

The advent of computer technology has brought a new level of expression to this addiction: addiction to the Internet. More specifically, the introduction of computer games to children and the Internet to adults provides a more fertile, and perhaps insidious, form of television addiction. A recent report described a mother whose children were taken into care. They were found unkempt, hungry and crying, smeared with their own faeces, whilst she plugged away for twelve to fourteen hours a day on the Worldwide Web.

Children whose intellect and brain functions are still in formation are particularly vulnerable to computer game addiction. The rise of attention deficit problems among school-age children may be directly related to exposure to computer games. More insidiously, lack of control over the level of exposure to these games may blunt the development of creativity and social skills, leaving the young person more prone to other kinds of addiction in later life.

Sex Addiction

Even more recent is the discovery that people can become addicted to sexual experiences. It may be that sexual addiction is a relatively new phenomenon, or that it has always existed and is only now coming to light. My view on the matter is that addictions in general are culture bound. This means that people tend to become addicted to substances and activities that have some cultural licence. Thus, for example, the Japanese are more likely to become addicted to amphetamines, the Chinese to opiates, and the Irish to alcohol. The sexual revolution in the 1960s and 1970s has now established itself as a more liberal and permissive view of sexual behaviour. Casual sex is now a social reality in most Western societies, and this licence allows a greater scope for addiction to develop.

Like most addictions, sexual addiction has certain defining characteristics. Sex addicts are compulsively engaged in the use of sexual experience for emotional distraction and relief. Their sexual behaviour has little or nothing to do with intimacy or relationship. Nor has it anything to do with the relatively-normal sexual needs that some people express by having a number of sexual partners, particularly during their early adult-hood. Rather, sex addiction is a compulsively-driven need to use sex to relieve the addict's sense of inner emptiness, or to alleviate feelings of anxiety or distress.

Modern society offers the sex addict an almost inexhaustible supply of sex-related stimulation. Sex toys, pornography and sex guides can all be used to intensify the creation of sexual excitement and relief. By tuning out of reality by consistently using fantasy and masturbation, drinking in the pictures and the stimulation, the sex addict gradually erodes any semblance of normal sexuality (which for most includes a certain level of fantasy and masturbation).

Eventually, the ability to experience true sexual love and intimacy is corrupted. Sex addicts confuse the biochemical sensations of sexual stimulation for the spiritual connection involved in sexual love. As the feelings of emptiness increase, the person tries harder to fill it with what is actually causing the emptiness, leading to the futile cycle that seems to be a central element in all addiction, namely using something to meet one's needs that can't do it, and that damages the person in the process.

Addiction to Work

Perhaps the most socially condoned and approved addiction is that which relates to work. It is a very common disorder which on the outside appears rather normal, but its effects are very destructive to any form of healthy, balanced life. Workaholics are those people whose existence becomes completely dominated by work. Many of the elements of other addictions described above also play a part in work addiction, and do not need to be repeated here. One aspect, however, that appears to be specific to this form of addiction is the need to secure the future through accumulation of wealth or assets. Work addicts are, in general, fearful of financial ruin, and through their great need to accumulate, some take major financial risks and end up in financial trouble anyway.

Insecurity is, then, a strong element in work addiction. Those close to the addict experience the loss of present-day security in the relationship, as the addict tries to make the future secure for his family. Many workaholics have come from backgrounds where there was financial worry, sometimes as a result of parental addiction, such as alcoholism. In their effort 'never to experience this again', they end up ruining their health and happiness through overwork.

Another strong element in workaholism is that of pride. Having experienced conditional love as a child, many work addicts believe that their worth is based on their career success and in the amount of money they make. Even as the wealth accumulates, the work addict cannot enjoy its benefits. Deeply unhappy within himself, his money cannot buy peace of mind, love or fulfilment. Each job well done and each substantial financial gain only gives a fleeting feeling of satisfaction, which must be repeated again and again. A stranger to his partner and children, the work addict strives harder and harder to find that elusive feeling of being a worthwhile human being.

Gradually, the years roll on, and the person finds himself more and more frustrated. Perhaps he experiences a traumatic mid-life crisis, underpinned by the recognition of reduced energy and of being overtaken by those younger than himself. In this case, the individual is prey to other forms of addiction, to sexual acting out or to major depression. The degree to which these storms are weathered are significant indications as to whether some form of physical, or mental, crisis will eventually overtake the person, leading to early death, suicide or emotional breakdown.

Religiosity

One message that emerges from the above is that most psychological addictions are the distortion of otherwise beneficial and healthy aspects of human life. Most good things can be used addictively — this also holds true of religion. In general, the religious ethos of a culture is regarded as the guardian of its moral values and ethics. Religion can, however, become a force for great destruction. Religious addiction has little to do with the great ethical statements of most religions. Rather, it is the use of religion as a method of rigid self-control, the suppression of life, a vehicle for prejudice and the harbinger of self-destructive guilt and shame. This form of religiosity has nothing to do with true spirituality, nor the belief systems that promote love, value and respect.

Religious addiction has several characteristics, and can be seen in a proportion of people in each major denomination. It has a different flavour, depending on whether it is rooted in a Judaeo-Christian or Islamic bent on the one hand, or the more esoteric and mystical focus of the East on the other. In the former, there is more likely to be a denial of feelings; a belief that authority is more important than relationship; a rigorous application of doctrinal law, with no reference to its relevance to a particular situation; and an alienation from all people who do not share the world view of the group. In the latter, the emphasis is on losing your ability to think, and giving up a sense of identity. Constant focus on tuning out of current difficulties leads to an inability to function, and a disconnection from others.

Religious addicts are, in general, idealistic, emotionally vulnerable people who fall prey to the promise of a particular group or system. They end up trying to contain their unhappiness and insecurity by wrapping it up in the certainties of their religious beliefs system, at the same time depending on the group members and leader for affirmation and emotional nurturing. This combination does not work, because on the one hand, reality has a way of insisting on being heard, and on the other, the group members are unable to give healthy nurturing, because they are too broken themselves.

Deeper dissatisfaction and distress is interpreted as not worshipping properly, or not being attentive to the rules, or not meditating properly, which leads to greater efforts and more soul searching. Anguish continues until the individual becomes a constricted, emotionally frozen tape-recorder, or gets the courage to leave the group. It is likely that on leaving he will fall foul of some other addiction, unless help is received. When this happens, it reinforces the other group members' beliefs that the world out there is evil, and that they should work hard at staying within the numbing embrace of their religious ideology.

Addictive Relationships

The notion that people can become psychologically addicted to another human being is a recent one, about which much is currently being written. The present description is the briefest of summaries of what is a complex and epidemic problem. In general, an addictive relationship is one in which an individual is: 1. consistently trying to change another person, in order to get their needs met; 2. being consistently hurt emotionally, and sometimes physically, in the relationship; 3. unable either to change their patterns, or leave the relationship.

People who are addictively involved with another person tend to show the following characteristics: low self-esteem; a high tolerance for suffering; a need to define one's worth in terms of other people's opinions; an overestimation of the suffering of others; an underestimation of others' ability to help themselves; and a sense of failure when one cannot make somebody else happy. All of these add up to a severe form of dysfunction, in terms of how to relate to oneself and others. In general, an addictive relationship is a mind-numbing, emotionally crippling, life-threatening condition.

Low self-esteem is the beginning of relationship addiction. This is usually a legacy of difficulty in childhood, when the child is treated badly; that is when he or she is unsupported, unloved and given little affection, admiration, praise or guidance. Some children will, as a result of these deficiencies, externalise their self-esteem into relationships. This means that they become completely dependent on the valuation of others in order to feel good about themselves. The periods of childhood and adolescence have, as their purpose, the formation of people whose sense of identity is intact, and who have a high level of love and respect for themselves. Without these positive formative influences, a person can wander through life desperately searching for somebody to give him that sense of self-esteem. As a result, such a person becomes a hostage to anyone who gives him praise or affection.

A person in an addictive relationship accepts the unacceptable. Having learned not to expect a lot from others, he is surprised when someone has a positive attitude towards him. The addictive person may marry the first person who shows any real interest, on that basis alone, and is consequently left struggling for years in a relationship that from the outset did not have what he needed, or even wanted. A high tolerance for suffering, and the capacity for endurance, often lead to a life of unhappiness and stress. Fear plays a significant part in addictive relationships. The stakes are very high — the needs for love and acceptance are intense, but are bounded by an equally intense fear of rejection.

People in addictive relationships do not have a secure sense of their own identity. They look outside themselves for a basis on which to gauge their worth. It is extremely difficult for them to risk rejection or criticism. This leads to perfectionist behaviour, and a high level of self-criticism. As a consequence, they set very high standards for themselves, usually are very responsible and hardworking, and will do anything rather than risk failure in their own eyes or those of their colleagues and friends.

This complex web of emotional traps is completed with an element of addictive relationship that leads many who suffer in this way to a lifetime of futility. This is their overweening sense of responsibility for the happiness of others, which afflicts them with enormous guilt in relation to how others feel. This guilt is grounded in an over-developed sense of responsibility for others. This message may have been imparted directly by parents, or indirectly by being exposed to the suffering of the parents.

All of these strands lead to an emotionally devastating way of living. In all major areas of life, including relationships to self, others and to work, relationship addicts are slowly spinning into a vortex of emotional, spiritual and intellectual exhaustion. Small wonder, then, that many find themselves gradually entrapped by some of the other types of addiction discussed above.

Summary

In this chapter, we have examined eight of the most common psychological addictions. Each has its own particular defining features, but they all share a common nature: people finding themselves in a compulsive cycle of using an activity to meet spiritual and emotional needs, to relieve pain and distress, in such a way that exacerbates the very problem it seeks to solve, and destroys the person in the process. These addictions are extremely powerful, and are sources of tremendous destruction to personal development and the ability to build a fulfilling life.

They also destroy the fabric of love relationships, and damage a parent's ability to help children to grow into healthy adults.

Through this destructiveness, these addictions also impact on the future of society. History tells us that some of the most magnificent societies and civilisations have been destroyed from the inside, by a variety of ideological or spiritual cancers. It is conceivable, therefore, that widespread addiction has the potential to destroy modern society. The next chapter examines some ways to deal with these problems.

CHAPTER 7

Key Elements in Recovery

Introduction

T he widespread growth of addiction has many political implications in terms of funding for health care, education and treatment. One issue of central importance is that of prevention. It is beyond the scope of this book to examine these matters, and I hope to address these questions in a later volume. Here, the focus is on presenting some useful information and guidance for people who are struggling in addiction, and for those who wish to help someone in this position.

In the next chapter, I will examine the major treatment approaches, and outline what I see as their strengths and weaknesses. Here, however, it seems useful to make some comments about the important elements involved in good recovery, regardless of the kind of treatment involved. This discussion is based on a wide variety of research and treatment outcomes, and suggests that there are several key areas that predict a good outcome for an individual struggling to deal with addiction.

Furthermore, it appears that treatment success is heavily influenced by the degree to which it includes or encourages the person to participate in all these elements. These key aspects are a willingness to change, detoxification, changing the environment, getting the right kind of support, working to plan, and undertaking long-term personal development.

Willingness to Change

One of the best-known books on the subject of alcoholism is *I'll Quit Tomorrow*. I like this title, because it captures one of the great difficulties that an individual encounters in the struggle with addiction. This difficulty refers to what it takes for the person to admit that he has a problem and needs to change. The willingness to change does not imply such complex motivations as wanting to change in order to be a better person, or to heal the damage to oneself or others. These are usually the reasons for staying clean and sober, rather than those that bring the person initially to confront his addiction.

For the most part, people in active addiction experience intense feelings of shame and guilt, and are thus highly unlikely to be driven to recovery by such noble feelings. The reasons that many people contemplate change are practical and immediate. It usually comes about because their addiction is threatening them with a substantial loss. Losing one's job, one's spouse, one's driving licence, one's house, or facing a term in prison, are all common motivations that bring people into the frame of mind where change is contemplated.

This type of motivation is called extrinsic motivation, which infers that desire to change is based on external factors. Extrinsic motivation is usually sufficient to help a person take the first steps towards recovery. It is very rarely sufficient to keep a person away from his addiction for any length of time, unless it is supplanted by intrinsic motivation. Intrinsic motivation refers to wanting change for reasons such as to be a better person, to be able to parent one's children properly, to be respected, to lead a productive life, and so on. Intrinsic motivation usually grows alongside recovery. The individual who is clean and sober begins to build a different set of values, and operates out of greater self-esteem and a more mature attitude to life.

A useful rule of thumb is that it doesn't matter what reason a person has to start recovery, as long at it begins the process. The individual might die before more noble reasons for change can emerge. This has significant implications for how to encourage someone to face up to an addiction problem. I will discuss this aspect in more detail in the next chapter. The desire to change, whether extrinsic or intrinsic, is essential to recovery. It is, however, only one strand in the cable of healing addiction, and rarely is sufficient by itself.

Detoxification

Detoxification is an important element of long-term healing from addiction. In the more commonly used sense of the word, it refers to a short time in hospital under sedation, while the body clears out the toxic drugs that the addict uses. That aspect is important, and useful for a minority of addicts who are usually in a chronic stage of addiction to mood-altering substances, such as alcohol or heroin. This is not the meaning in which I use it here.

Detoxification in the present context refers to a broader and much neglected aspect to the treatment and care of recovering addicts. Most people in addiction are seriously hindered by the toxins they carry around in their body. These toxins may be a result of a bad diet, lack of proper sleep and environmental damage, as much as to the drugs they take. A growing body of evidence shows that our emotional well-being is significantly related to the health of our bodies. When the body is in an unhealthy state, it is far more likely that our emotional well-being is easier to undermine.

To this finding we can add a profoundly significant fact: namely, that the strongest predictor of relapse in addiction is a negative emotional state. Thus, it is crucial for recovering addicts to protect their emotional integrity, if they are to stay clean and sober. One of the useful bits of advice that circulates among the Alcoholics Anonymous fellowship is that people need to be alert to the negative states of Hunger, Anger, Loneliness and Tiredness, or HALT for short. Negative emotional states have many causes, and are unavoidable in certain situations. However, when they are a direct result of a toxic build-up of chemicals in the body, then all the good intentions for sobriety will not solve this problem. Much help is now available in the areas of complementary medicine that is easily accessible in detoxifying the body, and thus negating this potential threat to sobriety.

Changing the Environment

Everything that people do occurs in a context. Most people have sex in bed, eat at table, go to work, wash in the bathroom, meet friends in familiar surroundings. For the most part, we are creatures of habit and we like certain consistencies in our day-to-day lives. Addicts are no different, and their addiction also happens in a context. This context includes the people they are with, the places they use, the sounds, tastes and feelings that occur when involved in the addictive activity. All of these begin to gain a certain power to trigger the need to act out the addiction. And it is extremely difficult for an addicted person to stop his addiction whilst remaining in the familiar addictive environment. The effects of environment cannot be underestimated in understanding addiction. It seems useful to briefly describe some of the more telling evidence in this regard.

Early this century, a Russian psychologist discovered that physical reactions that are not under conscious control can be triggered by circumstances that have no natural connection to those reactions. This information has profound implications for addiction. Pavlov used dogs in his experiments. When presented with food, a dog salivates automatically. When a bell was rung at the same time, the dog's physical system made a connection between the bell and salivating, so that after a certain number of sessions, the dog would salivate at the sound of the bell alone.

The important point here is that the dog did not sit back and think, 'Oh, I hear the bell, so the food must be coming, therefore, I must salivate.' What actually happens is that the bell — because it is now associated in the dog's nervous system with food — sends certain sound waves that enter the dog's central nervous system and trigger off the salivation response. This kind of learning is called conditioning, and it has been shown to be at work in the addictive process. Some examples will help to clarify this point.

During the Vietnam war, more and more American soldiers began to use drugs, so that in the later stages of the war a large number of GIs were using heroin regularly. There was great concern in the establishment that on their return, American society would face a drug problem of unprecedented proportions. Despite all the dire predictions, something very different happened. Of the soldiers who were habitual heroin users, ninety-two per cent had stopped using within one year of returning, most without any intervention. The remaining eight per cent matched exactly the number who used heroin before they joined the army.

This finding has many implications, but powerfully underpins the argument that environment plays a huge role in sustaining addiction. A young man who returns from the war to a small farm in the deep south will find it difficult to source heroin; additionally, he does not have to kill people as part of his day job, nor does he fear for his life. His friends down at the local bar are not users, so there is nothing to trigger a craving for the drug. These and many other changes in the environment made the task of quitting so much easier.

Most people who quit smoking can attest to the power of the environment in triggering the craving for a cigarette. An incident from my own experience comes to mind in this regard. Soon after I had stopped smoking, I was sitting in a hotel having watched my favourite soccer team lose an important game. During the game I was reasonably comfortable with not smoking. My brother arrived, and we decided to stay and chat. I ordered another pint, we sat down and he rolled up a cigarette.

As my brother continued talking, his voice seemed to be drifting away, and his cigarette seemed to get bigger and bigger; my conscious mind seemed to be taken over with a powerful sensation of desperately wanting to smoke. Before asking him for a smoke, I became aware of all the movement and sensations that would occur in taking a drag of the cigarette. I could feel it touching my lips, the slow seductive drawing in of the smoke, the dizzy sensation of the nicotine hit. I did it and it felt great. That was my last nicotine fix. (At least so far.)

Heroin addicts who are released from prison detoxified and drug free, can — often for years — experience an almost overwhelming desire to use the moment they find themselves in a familiar place where drug use is occurring. What is of great interest is that their brain chemistry reacts as if it has had a heroin fix, even when there is no drug present. Some of the treatments for addiction involve getting them to handle needles and the other accoutrements consistently without shooting up, to retrain their bodies away from the expectation that sets off the craving for the drug.

Many alcoholics can recount going into a bar and waking up several days later wondering what happened. These experiences have led some people to suggest that addicts are out of control. A more accurate view is that the individual is being unconsciously controlled by subtle but powerful cues that are setting off the addictive process. Part of my own work with recovering addicts involves helping them to deal with their relapses, or slips. I have yet to find that a relapse happens with no precipitating cause, and almost always there is some environmental impact at work.

In many cases, the individual is unaware of the forces that were at work leading up to the relapse.

All of these examples, and a great deal of other research, suggests that long-term recovery requires an understanding of environmental effects. In other words, the addicted person needs to become aware of the kinds of experiences — such as the tastes, smells, sounds, interactions, people and situations — that lead him back into addiction. There are no hard-and-fast rules that suit everybody and there are limits to how much change a person can make. That said, some changes to a person's environment are almost always a necessary part of recovery. I will give some specific guidelines in the next chapter.

Getting the Right Kind of Support

Very few people can make significant changes in their lives without the support or influence of others. Even the most resolutely independent people, who may believe that they have made their important decisions and life changes without recourse to others, have, in most cases, been influenced by those around them. It is a simple, logical step to accept that dealing with an addiction problem is better if positive influences from others can be brought to bear. Addicts who spurn the help of others have a poorer prognosis than those who can ask for and receive help and encouragement.

The key issue here is the right kind of support. An actively alcoholic doctor is unlikely to give the needed support to someone who has a drink problem. A food-addicted parent is less likely to help his or her anorexic daughter. A drug-dependent psychiatrist is less likely to confront the tranquilliser addict. Those who have an active addiction problem will be of little support to someone trying to recover. Rather, they will be more inclined to aid and abet the denial of others, by minimising the problem or explaining it away.

Where, then, does a person get the right kind of support? Two useful indicators are that the supporting person must care for the welfare of the addicted person, and must also know something about addiction. A caring spouse who reads up on the basic needs of addicts in recovery can be as important in helping the healing process as a professional counsellor, or a member of a support group. Perhaps the most likely area to get the right kind of support is among other people who are also in recovery from addiction. Such support is often available among recovery groups, including those recognised as twelve-step programmes. The success of these programmes is significantly related to the fellowship and support that the members provide for each other. There is more on this in the next chapter.

Working to a Plan

One of the defining characteristics of many addictions is that they lead a person into a life that becomes chaotic and unmanageable. The individual's emotional life is topsy-turvy, and he often feels like he is on an emotional roller-coaster. Finances are often affected, leading to worry and insecurity. Relationships suffer, and lack consistency. The early months of recovery work best if there is a plan that the individual can use to put structure and predictability into day-to-day living. Addicts often have great difficulty in tolerating boredom and ordinariness, and it is a part of being a healthy person to learn a degree of such tolerance. Constantly looking for a high, a buzz or a fix is not a healthy path to recovery.

My father once used a phrase that comes to mind. He was discussing how to cope with difficulty, and advised that we should learn how to 'do the menial task'. As the years have gone on, I have grown to see the wisdom in this approach. Sometimes during distress and difficulty, it is a great help to have some predictable task in which to involve oneself.

Working to a plan means designing a fairly rigid timetable of events that include work, recreational exercises and recovery activities. Such a plan can be built around the other elements I have discussed above, and could include activities that involve changing the environment, new hobbies and interests, getting support through new friends or support meetings, and so on. It may be useful to get help from a counsellor or support person in designing such a plan. Consistent effort to stay with it, as well as shaping it to suit particular needs, helps to give the individual some sense of order in life, as well as helping to cope with many of the insecurities and difficulties involved in early recovery.

Undertaking Long-Term Personal Development

Thus far, we have examined several key elements in recovery from addiction. It is clear that such recovery is not simply a matter of stopping an addictive activity. It also involves making fundamental changes to one's lifestyle and habit patterns. In order to proceed through the changes necessary to live well and healthily without recourse to addictive behaviour, most people require some long-term programme of personal development. Otherwise, people can kick one addictive habit only to find themselves continually frustrated and craving for the addictive substance, or simply replacing it with some other addiction.

Central to this argument is the belief that addiction masks personal difficulties, and prevents a person from maturing and living an emotionally healthy life. When the addiction is no longer active, the individual still has to face all the problems that were avoided through addiction. A good example is found among people who begin drinking heavily in late adolescence. Many such people live through their twenties and thirties in a fog of alcohol, and as a result did not grow through the developmental stages of early adulthood. When they stop drinking, many are still adolescents in their psychological maturity. In order to catch up to their developmental stage of middle adulthood, with its wisdom and responsibilities, they may need some guidance and counselling.

Commitment to long-term development is a crucial aspect of healing addiction. We have seen earlier that every person's addiction has a particular meaning, and is used for a particular purpose. These meanings and purposes may in fact be of real value, such as for spiritual experience, peace of mind or avoiding suffering. It is the use of addiction to achieve these ends that is destructive. Unless the individual discovers the meaning and purpose of the addiction, and finds new ways of achieving these purposes, then he will probably relapse, break down or live in chronic low-level misery.

Summary

This chapter examined what I consider to be the main elements in recovery from addiction. Every person's addiction is unique to him, and his recovery will involve some or all of these elements. The next chapter examines the kind of help that is available, and how such help can be used to include these areas of recovery.

CHAPTER 8

Getting the Help You Need

Introduction

I t is likely that the outside observer thinks of the helping professions as a rather benign group of people, hoping to do the best they can for the good of humanity. Within the field of addiction, one might consider this view to predominate — compassionate, intelligent people, striving toward a common goal of helping addicts to recover. What a lovely view this is — and what a pity that it does not reflect reality. Over the past fifty years or so, the field of addiction study and treatment has been marked out by political infighting, stubborn pride and arrogance among many of the helping services involved.

The central cause of these problems is the belief that there is one true answer to the problem of addiction. Different approaches have one thing in common: they have all asserted, at some time, that their view was the 'truth'. There is an old adage which says that 'when doctors differ, then patients die'. This is certainly true where addiction is concerned, and many have died because the professionals were too busy trying to prove the truth of their particular model, rather than seeking new and creative approaches to treatment. The 'truth' is that there are several approaches to the treatment of addiction; some work well for certain people and not so well for others. Different treatments have different success rates; none works for everybody, and most will work better than no treatment at all.

In this chapter, I will briefly examine the major options available to someone who wants help with an addiction. There are several major approaches available including medication; twelve-step support groups; individual or group counselling; hospital-based services; residential treatment in a specialist treatment centre; addiction rehabilitation centres; and what I call the do-it-yourself approach. Each area has its strengths and weaknesses, and each to some extent carries assumptions about the nature of addiction. In most cases, it is recommended that a person finds a suitable mix of treatment options that best suits their temperament and life situation.

Before discussing these options, it seems relevant to present some brief guidance to people who are concerned for someone who is in addiction. In general such people are the spouses, parents, family members, friends or colleagues of someone whose life is being damaged by drugs, alcohol or some other addiction.

Guidelines for Those who Care

Many people spend enormous energy, and become despairing and emotionally damaged, in fruitless efforts to help someone in addiction. This happens because they lack the insights needed to deal with this problem effectively. They rely on ordinary common sense, and a too optimistic belief in the force of reason and the power of love. The following suggestions are built around the two priorities that are essential to a healthy approach to addiction: protecting oneself and getting the addict to seek help.

1 Get assistance from an addiction counsellor — even one or two sessions can be a great help.
2 Join a support group for those whose lives are affected by a relationship with an addicted person (e.g. Al Anon or Nar Anon). You will need help and support in order to operate in the ways presented below.
3 Learn about addiction through reading and discussion. (My book *Children Under the Influence* examines in detail the

problems facing families, and gives comprehensive guidance on the matter.)

4 Do not enable the addict. Do not prevent him from experiencing the consequences of the addiction. Do not cover up for him, or make excuses on his behalf.

5 Do not discuss the problem while he is under the influence.

6 Do not nag, manipulate, ridicule, snipe at, demean or attack the addict.

7 If you are threatened, attacked or in danger, get out of the house and report it to the police.

8 Do not lend money for the addictive substance or activity.

9 Tell the addict that you are concerned and believe that help is needed. Do this once or twice, then leave it. Do not give this message in an angry or sarcastic way, or at an inappropriate time.

10 Plan to leave, or to ask the person to leave, if he does not get help. Living with an active addict who refuses to acknowledge the problem is a short way to a life of chronic misery and serious emotional damage. It prolongs the problems, creates havoc with children's emotional development, and gives the addict a false sense of security.

11 Do not make threats that you will not, or cannot, carry out. This destroys your credibility.

12 Always remember that you cannot change another person, but if you change yourself they may choose to change in response.

13 Do not keep the problem a secret — this will end up destroying you emotionally.

14 Recognise that in active addiction the normal rules of reason and moral conscience are being damaged. Appealing to reason and conscience is generally a waste of time. What you do is far more effective.

If you begin to use the above guidelines, the addict will be confronted with the need to get help much faster. The following is a description of the kinds of help available.

Medication

The use of medication to assist in the treatment of addiction has a very questionable history. Most of the drugs used to treat addiction are themselves addictive. We have seen earlier the devastating effects of using heroin to treat opium addiction, and the use of cocaine to treat morphine addiction. And in discussing their usage, it is important to make a distinction between what is called a harm reduction approach and a treatment approach. The use of methadone in helping heroin addicts is a good example of harm reduction. It is a highly toxic, addictive substance that is given under medical supervision to heroin addicts. The purpose is to help the heroin user minimise the risk of disease through dirty needles, and to avoid resorting to crime in order to get money to feed the habit. These approaches are important from a social and legal viewpoint, and include a tacit acceptance that some people who are addicted to heroin are going to stay actively addicted. It is not the function of this book to argue the effectiveness of this approach. It is discussed here to clarify the fact that reducing the harm associated with some addiction is not a treatment for the addiction itself. Thus, for example, the use of methadone is not a treatment for heroin addiction.

Recent focus on the biochemistry of addiction has, however, begun a new emphasis on the use of drug therapy as a direct treatment for addiction. The assumption underlying this approach is that addicts are suffering from a biochemical imbalance, that is causing their addiction. More specifically, a great deal of focus is being placed on the levels of dopamine and serotonin in the brains of addicts, whether they are alcoholics, gamblers, sex addicts or anorexics.

I have a deep scepticism towards this approach to addiction. I believe that it is, in part, an effort by the medical profession to be seen to provide an explanation — as well as gaining control of treatment — for what is an enormous social problem. There is a precedent for this. In the 1930s and 1940s, it became clear that the moral religious approaches to alcohol abuse were not working, and that the twelve-step approach — which saw alcoholism as a distinct progressive disease — had much to offer (one of the founder members of AA was a medical doctor). This approach was embraced by the medical establishment which, as a result, gained control of state funding on the one hand and payment by health insurers on the other for the medical treatment of alcoholism. The amounts of money involved are enormous.

It is understandable that the medical approach to alcoholism prevailed, because so little was understood about addiction at the time. Now, however, far more information is available, and it can be seen that despite the vast expenditure by medical and psychiatric services, alcoholism has not been shown to be a disease entity in the medical use of the word; nor does the more successful treatment of alcohol abuse involve medicine. I think it is important to learn from this historical precedent when the treatment of addiction is in question.

If medication is offered to someone in the grip of addiction, it is either seen as a method of harm reduction rather than a treatment (and as such may have some benefit); or it is a direct effort at treating the addiction. If it is seen as a treatment, then serious questions remain as to whether the assumptions under-lying this approach are secure. Treating gamblers with Prozac, and anorexics with similar medication, may take the focus off what is really going on in their addiction. It is a simple, neat philosophy, which to my mind is very premature and perhaps misleading. There may be a role for medication in a small percentage of cases. In general, however, it is best to await fur-ther support before embracing this treatment approach.

One other area where medication is used is as a means of either counteracting the effects of the addictive substance, or to make the person feel ill if taken in conjunction with the substance. A good example of the former is the use of Naloxone, which prevents the heroin user from experiencing the pleasant effects of heroin. The drug Disulfuram (antabuse) is an example of the latter, and makes a person very sick if he drinks an alcoholic beverage while it is present in his system. These drugs do not treat addiction; they make addiction uncomfortable, or prevent the drug taking effect. They have some benefit if taken by a highly motivated individual as a stop-gap measure to avoid relapse.

Twelve-Step Programmes

One of the most significant developments in the area of addiction treatment began in the 1930s, with the evolution of what is widely known as the twelve-step programme of Alcoholics Anonymous. This programme was developed over a period of years by two individuals — both serious alcohol abusers — a businessman named Bill Wilson and a doctor named Bob Smith. In their joint search for a way toward recovery from alcoholism, they devised a programme based on their own experiences, and incorporating the spiritual psychology of Carl Jung, and the writings of philosopher/educationalist William James, as well as the influence of the then current Christian evangelical renewal.

In the decades since then, the programme has developed and proliferated, and is now used as a basic model of recovery for a wide variety of addictions. These include gambling, drug addiction, eating disorders and relationship difficulties (particularly those concerned with relationships with addicts of one sort or another). Twelve-step programmes have been enormously beneficial, and to date have helped hundreds of thousands of people find a way back to sobriety and health.

On closer analysis, there are several reasons for the success of this model. Those who partake regularly in the programme experience three fundamental influences, outlined below.

Firstly, the programme is acknowledged as spiritual in nature, and the first step is concerned with the individual's recognition and acceptance of becoming powerless over a substance, or activity. This has the effect of encouraging the willingness to change, which we have discussed earlier as a key element in recovery. Addiction occurs when people give themselves up or over to the addictive substance or activity — it then takes control of their lives, and eventually destroys them if they do not find recovery. The twelve-step programme acknowledges this, and provides the possibility for the individual to supplant the activity by giving himself up or over to something else, a higher power, and to the programme itself. This can have a remarkably healing power.

A second strand in the effectiveness of these programmes is that of fellowship. The recovering individual is influenced and supported by the fellowship of others in a similar position as himself. The encouragement and, more crucially, the sense of identification, found among fellow members give a very positive basis for continuing sobriety. Added to this is the influence of what is called sponsorship, whereby an individual with a long period of sobriety takes the role of sponsor, or mentor, with a newly recovering addict. The healthy example provided, as well as advice and support, has often helped a new member from returning to addiction in moments of crisis.

Thirdly, a change of environment and lifestyle (crucial elements in recovering from addiction) is made possible by partaking in the programme. Most addicts have consistent and habitual ways of acting out their addiction. Frequenting particular pubs or betting shops, and the company of a set of equally sick companions, make it very difficult for them to cease their addiction. Being part of a fellowship provides new avenues to friendship and different recreational patterns — the bowling alley and coffee mornings replace the card table and the pub. Additionally, twelve-step meetings are easily accessible and are free. Anyone struggling in addiction, who wants help, would be well advised to give them a try.

Twelve-step programmes have some limitations. In general, it can be said that when an addiction grows out of the pain of a damaged and hurt person, the programme — whilst providing much by way of helping that person stay sober and learn a new way of living — will not be able to address the deeper needs for healing. Rather, the person may stay away from the primary addiction, only to find himself addicted to something new, including perhaps an addiction to the fellowship itself. This is shown in the numbers who spend decades in the fellowship, but seem to go around in circles, continually telling the same old stories and showing little in the quality of their lives that suggests they are getting any better.

For a significant number of recovering addicts, much of the damage to their personalities will have been covered up through addiction, and is often outside of conscious awareness. It may take some period in counselling, combined with continued involvement in the fellowship, to get beyond the cycle of being stuck at a particular place of being dry, or clean, but not sober and healthy.

Another limitation of the programme is that some people find the spiritual emphasis very difficult to embrace. Those who use the programme have already taken on the mantle of a particular version of the spiritual way of life, and there is in some cases a certain arrogance that exists in any ideologically-based group. Everybody who succeeds through the programme is a living advertisement for its success. Those who don't succeed and find no other help will usually die, and their voice is left unheard. Why they could not benefit from the programme, or the blocks that prevented them from healing, are left unknown. With this qualification, we can still acknowledge that twelve-step programmes are a very powerful and effective source of healing and recovery for many people. I do not, however, believe that they are the only way to health and sobriety.

Addiction Treatment Centres

Residential treatment for addiction has become very common in the past twenty-five years. The most common model used in this approach is called the Minnesota Model. This model was born out of the twelve-step movement, when a group of re-covering alcoholics set up a centre to encourage others to join with them in attempting recovery in a peaceful setting away from their usual environment. The treatment approach usually involves a four- to six-week residential programme, that combines the twelve-step approach with other forms of counselling and group therapy. Of particular significance is the therapy model called Reality Therapy. This is a practical, behaviour-focused model, developed by William Glasser, and is useful as a means of assisting a person to recognise how he is dealing with his life. (It is, in my opinion, seriously deficient as a model of long-term personal growth, but that is not particularly relevant in the early stage of treatment.) These programmes are, in general, privately run concerns offering a range of professional intervention.

One of the major advantages of a treatment centre approach lies in the fact that those concerned for the addict can access help through these agencies and learn how to deal with the addict differently, so as to encourage entry to treatment. By making contact with a treatment centre, an individual can be advised as to how to encourage the addict to get into treatment. This means that the addict may get into recovery faster than if left to 'bottom out' and join a programme of his own accord.

Treatment centres vary in their success rates, and anyone close to the issue of addiction realises that there will be a percentage of addicts who will not recover, no matter what happens to them. The decision to undertake treatment for addiction at a treatment centre is a difficult one for many people. In general, if after trying through a twelve-step programme, and on the advice of professionals familiar with the problem of addiction, an individual is unable to abstain or control his habit, then it may be the best option.

The strengths of a good residential treatment complement that of the twelve-step programme in the following ways. It takes the person out of his usual environment and provides him with a drug- or activity-free context in which to take stock of his life. It provides support and identification through the other members of the treatment group. It provides counselling and education that help speed up his self-understanding. Most importantly, it provides weekly after-care group meetings, once the individual has successfully completed the residential period of treatment.

Irish treatment centres report an astoundingly high success rate relative to those in Europe or the United States. The two best-known centres, the Rutland Centre in Dublin and Aiseiri in County Tipperary, report success rates of between sixty and seventy per cent for clients who complete their programmes. Success is defined as being consistently abstinent from the drug or activity for one complete year after leaving treatment. This statistic is very encouraging in terms of the quality of care being offered. It can be said, however, that there may be some additional reason for this level of success. It is difficult to accept that treatment centres in Europe and the United States are not doing as good a job. Their success rates are generally between thirty and fifty per cent. One factor that may explain the differing success rates is the availability of aftercare group therapy provided by the treatment centre. Ireland, being a geographically small country, allows those clients who complete the residential part of treatment to access the aftercare provided by the treatment centre they attended. By doing so, they keep links with others who were in treatment at the same time, thus forging stronger bonds, a firmer support network, and a greater level of accountability. As we have seen earlier, these factors are strongly related to recovery outcome.

Another, and perhaps less obvious, factor may have something to do with the deeply ingrained Catholic ethos in the Irish
psyche, which makes people more accessible to the spiritual
underpinnings of treatment centre ideology. Whatever the
reasons (some of which annoy certain people in the treatment
field), these success levels are indeed encouraging.

One criticism that has been levelled at residential treatment (particularly at those that adhere to the Minnesota
Model) deserves note. Because it is an intensive and relatively
short-term treatment, there is a tendency to apply the model to
all people as if each addict was not a unique individual whose
addiction has its own unique story and root cause. One particular aspect has come in for questioning in this regard. This
concerns the role of denial. It is a reality that most people who
suffer from addiction are in denial, and require 'help' in order
to break through their defences. In a zeal to accomplish this
task, there have been situations where the confrontation of the
addict has taken such a form that some suffered unnecessarily
and in some cases needed help to heal the wounds visited upon
them by over-zealous practitioners, who mistook the addiction
for the person and lost sight of the fact that some addicts are
the most sensitive and gentle people in the world. Thankfully,
there is, in the Irish treatment centre context, a growing
rejection of these over-confrontational approaches to those in
addiction, and a greater recognition that it is the person — and
not the addiction — that is being treated.

Counselling

The field of counselling and psychotherapy has come in for some
severe criticism in relation to its approach to addiction. Much of
this criticism is justified. Many counsellors who are schooled in
the classical therapy models of psychoanalysis, cognitive therapy
and others do not have a specific training in the field of addiction.
They tend to use their therapeutic approach inappropriately, in

the belief that addiction responds to therapy in a similar fashion to other human problems. This is not the case. Nor is the widespread notion that addiction is simply a symptom of other psychological problems an acceptable orientation. As a result, many active addicts — especially those with addiction problems — spend their time going from one therapist or psychiatrist to another, often for years, trying to sort out all the psychological bugbears that are afflicting their lives, with no hope of recovery until the addiction problem is addressed. Because of their training and ideological stance, the best intentioned and most skilful therapist may miss this essential point.

More recent developments in the field of counselling have given greater attention to the specific problems associated with addiction. Furthermore, there is now a branch of counselling devoted specifically to addiction, and some counsellors specialise in this field. These are known as addiction counsellors and are, at least initially, a better option for someone with an addiction problem. I say initially because, in my opinion, there is a problem in the field of addiction counsellor training. On its own, it is too narrow in focus. Whilst addiction should not be reduced to something else, and needs to have specific therapeutic efforts addressed to its nature and its place in a person's life, neither can it be separated completely from many of the other aspects of the person's psychological and spiritual nature. Thus, for long-term recovery, it would appear that counselling is best provided by someone who has in-depth experience and training in many aspects of human psychology, but who also has specific exposure to addiction and its treatment.

Hospital-Based Treatment

State and private health services are being expanded to deal with the issue of addiction. This is in response to both the growing incidence of addiction problems, and it being more clearly recognised as a specific health problem in its own right.

Consequently, more and more hospitals are offering services to those with addiction problems. The focus is still primarily on the treatment of alcoholism, because it continues to be the most destructive and widespread addiction in Ireland.

Hospital-based services are quite varied. Some provide a detoxification service and include a short residential programme. Others place the emphasis on an out-patient programme that incorporates group therapy, individual counselling and rehabilitation activities. Some encourage patients to attend a twelve-step programme such as Alcoholics Anonymous. Others favour retraining the patient towards controlling his substance use. There is continued expansion of these services, and the focus appears to be moving away from residential treatment and more towards out-patient care.

The strengths of an out-patient approach are that it is more accessible to a larger number of people, and perhaps can reach the individual earlier in the addictive process. A person in early-stage addiction is, in my opinion, far more likely to visit an out-patient counselling service, than to sign in for a six-week intensive residential programme. On the other hand, the out-patient approach can place a very heavy burden on some patients who have no respite from the environmental cues that trigger the addiction. For some addicts, these problems and environmental triggers feel insurmountable, and they might do better having a break away from the everyday environment until some recovery work has had a chance to take hold.

Rehabilitation Centres

These differ from the treatment centres described above. The focus is on long-term rehabilitation, rather than short-term intensive treatment, and clients tend to stay for periods up to a year. Rehabilitation centres provide individuals with a safe environment and a support network whilst they try to rebuild their lives. They are encouraged to forge links to the community through work and social connection. Participants live at the centre and take responsibility for day-to-day domestic tasks, thus re-learning, in many cases, the basic skills of looking after themselves and of taking responsibility. Participants are expected to partake in a twelve-step programme as a central part of their recovery.

These centres are not funded by private insurance, and do not engage in the intensive therapy found in a residential programme. Many people who make use of these centres could not afford to enter private treatment. Many are deprived through their addiction, but also through the very real social impoverishment that is often a major causal factor in the development of addiction. In general, the average stay at such a centre ranges from several months to a year.

The Do-it-Yourself Approach

We have seen earlier that very few people achieve anything of significance in life solely on their own. Inability to trust, a strong ego, or fundamental insecurity often lead people to believe that they are more independent than they actually are. That said, some people are more independent than others — it is simply a matter of degree. Those more independent types who also have an addiction problem may be attracted to the notion that they will beat their addiction on their own. Good examples of this approach are found amongst the millions of people who succeed in giving up smoking. Of all addictions, cigarette smoking is one of the most endemic and difficult to beat.

The do-it-yourself approach is defined here as quitting an addiction without engaging professional help or joining a recovery programme. Whilst it is a path fraught with difficulty, it is possible for some people; certain addictions are also more accessible to this approach than others. The following is some strategic advice, based on the key elements of recovery discussed in the previous chapter.

Prepare to Stop

This stage involves preparing one's mind for the day you will quit. Take a month to do this. In this period, read some books on the topic of addiction. List reasons for stopping, and programme your mind by repeating some of these reasons every day. Set a target date for stopping, and tell your friends your decision.

Change the Way and Amount you Use

During the preparation stage, start cutting down, but do not let yourself be seduced into the notion that you will gradually cut out the habit. Use the cutting-down period to strengthen your resolve, and tell yourself that it will help lessen withdrawal when D-Day arrives. Cutting down means using less, so postpone the first dose, or take it later than usual. Set an upper limit each day.

Change the setting in which you use your drug, by making it less pleasant. If you like using in company, then do it alone. Break the situational temptations by avoiding use in more pleasant surroundings. Acknowledge that you are an addict, and try to take any romance out of the situation. Set up a more active schedule in your life. Build in activities that have no connection to your drug use, such as evening classes, hobbies or charity work.

D-Day

On the day you quit, remind yourself of the following:

◆ quitting is possible, and thousands of people do it successfully

◆ you owe it to yourself not to be a slave to a substance, or activity

◆ withdrawal symptoms are temporary, and will ease soon

◆ if you relapse, you have to start all over again

◆ one use will lead to another

◆ for someone who has an addiction problem, there is no such thing as one drink, cigarette, bet or fix; this is a very important affirmation, because the temptation is almost always couched in terms of 'just one'

◆ write these down on an index card, and carry it around and read it every hour.

Do the Following:

◆ each day, tell someone that you have stayed clean
◆ do not lie
◆ use a relaxation method, such as breathing exercises, to music each morning
◆ stay away from tempting environments
◆ review your list of reasons for wanting to quit
◆ talk about non-use to friends and relatives, and enlist their support
◆ distract yourself by doing something during a craving experience, rather than analyse your feelings
◆ if you slip, do not use it as an excuse for complete relapse
◆ get some physical exercise each day.

This do-it-yourself approach does not address the causes for addiction; nor does it address the void that is often left in the life of a recovering addict. It is presented here as a simple guide to those who wish to try this method. In my own experience with recovering addicts, it will work for some, but many do better in a more structured approach. It can, however, be incorporated into an individual's use of other resources — such as following a twelve-step programme or attending counselling — and is perhaps best used in that context.

Summary

This chapter has presented some brief guidance to those who are concerned for someone who has an addiction problem. It also examined some of the most common forms of treatment available. For many people, the approach that works best involves a combination of treatment approaches, in conjunction with family members also taking on the challenge of change. The next chapter presents some useful resources where help can be accessed.

C H A P T E R   9

Useful Resources

Introduction

At last the problem of addiction is getting the attention it deserves. It is being seen more clearly as an endemic problem of society that afflicts people of all ages and in all walks of life. It exists, albeit in different forms, in mansions of the wealthy, churches of all denominations, middle-class suburbia and the tenements of the poor. It is not limited to the disadvantaged or the undeveloped, although poverty and educational disadvantage do provide a more fertile ground for its widespread growth. We still have a long way to go to understand its nature fully, but we do know that the sooner help is received, the better for the afflicted person, friends and family, and ultimately society.

Below is a brief listing of some helpful resources. A more comprehensive listing that includes treatment and counselling in the United Kingdom, has been compiled by the Catholic Church and is published in the magazine *Intercom*, May 1997. Back issues can be ordered through your local newsagent.

Twelve-Step Programmes

Attending a twelve-step meeting is, for some people, a daunting task. Images from television soap operas of sitting in a crowded room and announcing to the world that you are an addict tend to delay many people from attending. Difficulty with the concept of admitting anything is also a problem. It is useful to remember that the only requirement for going to a twelve-step meeting is a desire to stop a particular activity, e.g. drinking, gambling, overeating, etc. It doesn't matter what you believe about the problem. And you will not be asked to speak. You can just go and watch, and listen. It is that simple. Meetings are held regularly, and information about location and times can be accessed by telephone. Relevant numbers are as follows:

Alcoholics Anonymous: 01 453 8998.
Al Anon (family support): 01 873 2699.
Gamblers Anonymous: 01 872 1133.
Narcotics Anonymous: 01 830 0944.
Nar Anon (family support): 01 874 8431.
Sexaholics Anonymous, PO Box 92, Waterford.
Overeaters Anonymous: 01 451 5138.

Hospital-Based Addiction Services

A growing number of hospitals provide addiction treatment and a counselling service. Many of these deal primarily with alcohol abuse. These include in-patient and out-patient services throughout the country. They can be accessed through referral from your general practitioner, or through the reception services of most hospitals. A listing of all the various services is too cumbersome here. The best-known private psychiatric hospitals are:

St John of God's
Stillorgan, Co. Dublin. Tel. 01 288 1781.

St Patrick's Hospital
Steeven's Lane, James's Street, Dublin 8.
  Tel. 01 677 5423.

Residential Treatment Centres

Treatment centres offer a four- to six-week residential programme to suitable candidates for treatment of drug addiction, alcoholism and gambling. The procedure is relatively simple. An appointment is made by telephone for an assessment. The person attends the appointment usually with a family member, and is met by a trained counsellor who helps to assess whether the person needs treatment, and if the programme is appropriate to his needs. A date is then set for entering treatment.

The programme itself incorporates group therapy, family intervention and other activities. On completing the programme, the individual is expected to attend weekly after-care meetings for up to two years, as well as attending a twelve-step programme. Most are covered by private health insurance.

Aiseiri, Cahir, Co. Tipperary. Tel. 053 41818.

Aiseiri, Roxborough, Wexford. Tel. 052 41166.

Bushypark Treatment Centre, Ennis, Co. Clare.
  Tel. 065 40944.

Hope House, Foxford, Co. Mayo. Tel. 094 56888.

Rutland Centre, Templeogue, Dublin 16. Tel. 01 494 6358.

Tabor Lodge Treatment Centre, Ballindeasig, Belgooly,
  Co. Cork. Tel. 021 887110.

Talbot Grove, Castleisland, Co. Kerry. Tel. 066 41511.

Addiction Counselling

We have seen earlier that addiction counselling differs from much of the counselling presently available; it is important to clarify that a counsellor has some specific experience in dealing with the problem of addiction. One way to simplify this is to contact a counsellor through an addiction treatment body — either a treatment centre or a community-based group that is involved with addiction. The following is a brief listing.

Community Addiction Counselling Services in Dublin

Dun Laoghaire. Tel. 01 280 8471.

Castle Street, Dublin 2. Tel. 01 475 7837.

Main Street, Tallaght. Tel. 01 451 5397.

Rathdown Road, Dublin 7. Tel. 01 838 9326.

Edenmore Park, Raheny, Dublin 5. Tel. 01 848 0666.

Ballymun, Dublin 11. Tel. 01 842 0011.

Addiction Information Centre, Farmhill Road, Goatstown, Dublin 14. Tel. 01 298 8983.

Community Alcohol and Drug Services outside Dublin

Portlaoise, Co. Laois. Tel. 0502 21634, Ext. 409.

Mullingar, Co. Westmeath. Tel. 044 48289.

St Mels Road, Longford. Tel. 043 46827.

St Vincent's Hospital, Athlone, Co. Westmeath. Tel. 0902 74028.

Any of these numbers can be contacted for information regarding addiction counselling.

Rehabilitation Centres

Initial contact is usually made by telephone, and an assessment procedure similar to the treatment centre approach is set up.

Alcoholic Rehabilitation Centre

19 Nassau Street, Dublin 2. Tel. 01 454 3793.

Coolmine Therapeutic Community

Lord Edward Street, Dublin 2. Tel. 01 679 7830.

Cuan Mhuire

Turloughmore, Galway. Tel. 091 797102.

Cuan Mhuire

Milltown, Athy, Co. Kildare. Tel. 0507 31090.

Cuan Mhuire

Newry, Co. Down. Tel. 080693 69121.

Marist Rehabilitation Centre

Retreat Road, Athlone, Co. Westmeath. Tel. 0902 72035.

Horizon House

Cappagh Road, Galway. Tel. 091 591812.

Further Reading

Buckroyd, Julia, *Eating Your Heart Out: Understanding and Overcoming Eating Disorders*, London: Vermilion 1996.

An excellent overview of eating disorders and useful guidance for recovery.

Carr, Allen, *The Easy Way to Stop Smoking*, Harmondsworth: Penguin 1991.

A very practical and useful approach to giving up smoking.

Hardiman, Michael, *Children Under the Influence*, Cork: Paragon Books 1993.

By mail order at tel. 0902 79062. An insightful and readable account of how families are affected by parental addiction (particularly alcohol abuse), with specific guidance for change and recovery.

Johnson, Vernon, *I'll Quit Tomorrow*, New York: Harper & Row 1973.

A useful introduction to the abstinence approach to recovery from alcoholism.

McNamara, Mary, *The Psychology of Addiction*, London: Taylor & Francis 1990.

Scholarly and well-researched guidebook to the psychological approaches to understanding and treating addiction.

Plagenhoef, Richard L. and Carol Adler, *Why Am I Still Addicted: A Holistic Approach to Recovery*, Whitby, Ontario: TAB 1992.

A very informative guide to healing the body and mind from influences that support or encourage addiction.

Index